LAUGH 'N SCRATCH

To
Allison
as promised.

Not quite Dorothy Whipple
but trying hard

with very best wishes
from

Peter S Farley

06 - VIII - 2018

PETER S FARLEY

Dedicated to
Andrew William Farley
for encouraging me
to write this story

This novel is entirely a work of fiction. The names, characters and incidents portrayed in it are the work of the author's imagination. Any resemblance to actual persons, living or dead, events or localities is entirely coincidental.

A catalogue record for this book is available from the British library.
ISBN N0: 978-0-9932824-3-0

Published by: www.grandpatravels.com
First printing: 2018

Other titles by this author are:

Mysterious Tales from Turton Tower
The Red Tabs
A Pensioner Visits Peru

Each title may be obtained from:
peterfarley@hotmail.com
or
www.grandpatravels.com

FOREWORD

This story is about a 1960s English cinema. Its name *Majestic* was displayed above a Romanesque styled entrance. A stone column stood at each end of three long marble steps. Inside the foyer were mahogany wooden kiosks. They housed staff members who collected entrance fees from the visiting patrons. Beyond the foyer was a spacious auditorium. It sported a singular wide balcony. Each entrance door was guarded by a member of staff. Entry was gained by producing a serial numbered ticket. The guardian tore the ticket into two halves. One of which was kept by the patron, as proof of payment. The other half was carefully pricked by what resembled a short darning needle. The needle being attached to a piece of string. The half ticket was pushed along the string and retained. At the end of the show the manager collected the half-tickets from both balcony and auditorium. Once counted their total monetary value was expected to equal the cash takings at the kiosks. The auditorium was lit by large circular fittings let into its ceiling. At floor level seating of the flip-up type was placed in successive rows.

They were generally known as the 'stalls.'

Each faced towards an elevated stage. The backdrop to the stage was a projection screen in front of which were fabric curtains. The screen acted as an imaginary window through which a fantasy world could be viewed. Albeit the world was created by the projected images from celluloid film. Vertical shafts of light illuminated the lower part of the curtains. Its effect formed part of a created mystique. At the start of the show the lighting was slowly extinguished. Soon afterwards a shaft of light from a huge film projector left the projection room. Travelling through the air it fell onto the curtains which opened without any apparent assistance. They exposed the giant reflective screen that suddenly became 'alive' with moving images. The fantasy world had been revealed.

The cinema's main function was to provide entertainment but there was something more. It offered sanctuary to those seeking refuge from the 'real' world. By entering its doors the cinemagoer could be absorbed by the illusion of an imaginary world. Personal worries could be forgotten. At least for a few precious minutes.

CHAPTER ONE

January was a particularly cold month. A weather forecast predicted heavy falls of snow over England. Cold and damp air drifted across a Lancashire cotton town. The roof slates of the old mill houses glistened with deposited moisture. Spirals of smoke rose from their short chimney stacks. They provided a clue that the houses were inhabited.

A pair of large brown eyes gazed into a mirror that hung above an open fireplace. They took in the reflected image of a well groomed teenager. He had recently celebrated his fifteenth birthday and took pride in wearing his presents. They were the latest two piece Italian-styled suit and a pair of chistle-toed leather shoes. It was 1963 and the clothes were the height of fashion. At either side of the fireplace were cloth-covered armchairs. The boy's parents had carefully placed them to face the steadily burning coal fire. His mother looked up from reading her book. She gazed at him admiringly and offered some words of advice.

"Now then Stuart, 'ave you got a clean 'ankerchief an' some money for t' bus in case it rains?"Combing some hair away from his forehead he replied rather tiredly. "Yes, mother".

He knew she meant well but now and again he resented her fussing.

A large opened newspaper was held above the opposite arm-chair. A disembodied voice called out from behind it. "Why, where's he goin'?" inquired the boy's father.

"I'm startin' that job at cinema dad" revealed Stuart.

The newspaper was slowly lowered to expose a bespectacled and balding, middle-aged man. He suddenly remembered he had seen a vacancy for a projectionist at the local cinema. It had been advertised in his newspaper a week or two ago.

"Oh so you got that job at laugh 'n' scratch did you?"

His father looked him over and before Stuart could reply he uttered a second question.

"As thee got them new square-toed shoes on? Them as yer aunt bought thee. I likes them I do. They let you get nearer t' bar int' pub, when beer's bein' served".

He chuckled aloud thinking he was being funny but called out to his wife for ratification. "I'nt that right love? "

Stuart's mother nodded with a look of mild

indifference. Turning to Stuart she said,
"Take no notice of him son, you get off now an' don't be late home."

Stuart nodded in affirmation but looking puzzled he asked a question.

"What does dad mean when he says 'laugh and scratch'?"

"Oh," started his mother. "When your dad and me went t' pictures years ago, things were different. They used to say that seatin' inside cinema were none too clean. Due to that it carried a few fleas. When pictures were shown on t' screen sometimes we laughed. At same time we was scratchin' from t' fleas that were on t' seats! That's why we called cinema 'laugh n scratch'!

Stuart's mother instantly lowered the tone of her voice.

"But that's all changed now" she said.

The parents looked at each other knowingly and chuckled. Stuart shrugged his shoulders and after straightening his tie turned to leave the room.

Outside the house, Stuart walked at a brisk pace along the dark and hushed streets. The stone flagged pavements were wet and dirty. His feet instinctively side-stepped a puddle. The water shone like a mirror, as it reflected light from a nearby street lamp. He glanced at his wrist watch and muttered "I'm making good time." Laughingly he added "No pun intended of course."

His mother had bought the watch to complement his new suit. It fitted him perfectly and its fabric-covered buttons added a touch of professionalism. Stuart especially liked how they fastened high on his chest. The arrangement seemed to accentuate the presence of his dark blue tie. Although the weather was particularly cold he hadn't noticed. Maybe it was the thickness of his suit's material. Or was it the prospect of starting a new job?

As he approached the town's centre he could see the cinema in the distance. Perhaps because it was late on Saturday afternoon there appeared to be few people around. Stuart reasoned that the shoppers having bought their goods had gone home. A couple of hours would pass before the next wave of people descended on the centre. They would be the revellers seeking entertainment either in the public houses or the cinema.

The central market hall stood silent and proud. Its tall clock tower displayed four faces of time. Stuart's wrist watch compared favourably with them. His appointment with the cinema's manager was for five o'clock. He had one minute to spare. Approaching the cinema Stuart caught sight of the name *Majestic*. It was embossed on marble tiles and displayed like a beacon high above the entrance. His eyes slowly descended. They stopped and refocused when they saw a solitary man.

Standing at the top of three marble steps he presented himself as a tall and slimly built figure. He wore a grey double-breasted pin-striped suit. It was complemented by a tired looking shirt. Their style suggested they had been bought at the end of World War Two. But the addition of a bright blue tie gave his persona a touch of modernity.

His head was covered with thick black hair. It was liberally treated with brilliantine with the sides rigidly slicked back. They met in the nape of his neck. But some noticeable groups of grey hairs seemed to defy explanation. They suggested he was either older than his looks or he had experienced a strife punctuated life.

Standing upright in military fashion his hands were clasped behind his back.

He contemplated a kaleidoscope of sounds and shapes that appeared before him. Public transport buses and motor cars passed at a distance. People too were making their way homewards. They appeared like refugees from a shopping expedition. He surveyed everything as though it was his kingdom. Imagining himself to be a king and the people his loyal subjects. Ironically though, a cigarette dangling from the corner of his mouth lessened the illusion of his regal status!

A voice called out. "Excuse me sir, are you Mister Thompson the manager?"

The man stiffened as though he was poked in the ribs. His hand rose quickly to his mouth and took hold of the cigarette. He looked down from his elevated position. Stuart was gazing at him with his bright smiling face.

"Aye, I am lad. Are you Stuart?"

"Yes sir. I've come about the projectionist job."

The manager looked Stuart up and down.

"Aye lad" he said "I've been expecting you. You're on time; that's good. Come on up!"

The manager turned around and opened a glass-panelled mahogany door.

Stuart strode up the marble steps as quickly as he could. He took care not to slip. He was mindful that his leather-soled shoes were still new and shiny. The manager held the door open.

"Come in lad" he said "Follow me and we'll have a chat in my office."

He locked the door behind them and strode across the foyer. The evening show was expected to start within the next couple of hours.

The manager's office was strategically placed at the foot of a stairwell. Its stairs led to the balcony area and beyond that was the projection room. Facing the office door were two pay kiosks that dominated the foyer's entrance area.

The office was a small oblong room. It contained a quaint roll-top wooden desk. At each end of the desk stood a chair made from matching wood. Somehow the limited space managed to accommodate everything.

"Sit down in that chair lad" said the manager, pointing to the chair nearest the office door. He placed his still burning cigarette into his mouth. Using both hands he pushed open the desk's roll-top. To the untrained eye the desk was filled with clutter. But there was one item that took precedence over everything else. It was a large glass ash tray. The manager stumped his cigarette into its base. He killed all traces of its life.

"A filthy habit" he admitted aloud, "But one that I have no intention of changing."

The manager sat in the opposite chair and looked across at Stuart. He saw him surveying the contents of his desk.

"It's a bit of a mess lad but at least I know where everything is!"

Stuart had noticed a small framed photograph of a wedding couple. The groom looked like a younger version of Mister Thompson. Even his suit resembled the one the manager was presently wearing.

Stuart instantly chose not to mention it. Instead he chirped, "Oh, no sir, I just happened to notice the medals there. My dad has got one of those."

The manager's face brightened. He reached forward into the desk and picked up a star-shaped copper medal. Embossed on its face were the words 'The Africa Star'. He held it aloft by its multi coloured ribbon.

"Do you mean this one?" he asked.

"Yes Mister Thompson, that's it."

The manager's countenance instantly changed to one of questioning surprise.

His voice took on an air of excitement.

"Did your father say what places he got to during the war?"

Stuart nodded vigorously.

"Oh yes sir. My dad said he was in North Africa and at the famous battle of El Alamein." The manager's face lit up.

"Well I never! That's where I was. We might even have been in the same mob."

He paused for a moment and then admitted, "We have something in common lad."

Quickly directing his eyes towards Stuart's chest he declared "And I notice we are wearing the same colour of tie!"

At this moment if any proverbial ice needed to be broken, it would surely be in splinters!

Within seconds the mood changed when the manager asked another question.

"Now then lad, what do you know about moving pictures?"

"Well, I enjoy watching them sir, but I don't know much about how they're made."

The manager continued. "And what about showing moving pictures to the public?"

"I know even less" admitted Stuart.

"What films do you like to watch?"

Stuart thought for a few moments. He looked at the floor hoping to find some inspiration. Suddenly he remembered.

"Oh yes, I like Laurel and Hardy films; they're my favourites."

"Good choice!" exclaimed the manager.

A knowing smile appeared on his face.

"Did you know that Stan Laurel was a lad from Lancashire?"

Stuart silently shook his head.

"Aye, he was" assured the manager.

"He lived a few miles from here up int' Lake District. His father was a theatre manager you know?"

Stuart remained silent. The manager pointed to a large paper poster. It was stuck to the wall above his desk. Printed on it was a colourful image of an adult couple. They were shown to be embracing. Superimposed across the image were the bold words 'Gone with the Wind.'

He asked a rhetorical question. "Do you see that poster there?"

They both looked with interest towards the wall.

"That's one of the great films of the 1940's. The figures are Clark Gable and Vivien Leigh who were both famous film stars."

The manager observed Stuart's response. He appeared not to be particularly moved.

"Anyway" said the manager, wishing to regain control of the moment, "I would like you to stare at that poster for a minute."

"Do you mean like this?" asked Stuart.

Stuart turned his head and forcibly fixed his opened eyes on the print.

"That's right" encouraged the manager.

"And when I tell you to, but not before, I want you to close your eyes."

He saw that Stuart's gaze was fixed on the poster.

"This is one film you will never forget in years to come" he remarked.

After the mandatory minute had expired, the manager's voice barked,

"Right! Stop! Now close your eyes lad."

Stuart complied with the command. Following a brief pause the manager said,

"Okay lad. Now without opening your eyes tell me what you can see."

Stuart described with alacrity the vision he witnessed.

There were two embracing figures and printed words in bold type. They were all so clear to him and all the while his eyes remained closed.

"Very good" said the manager, "You can open your eyes now."

The manager was watching him intently. Stuart opened his eyes and blinked a few times. Within seconds he was composed.

His eyes had readjusted to the room's lighting.

"That is what is known as *persistence of vision*" explained the manager. "It's a condition of our eyesight. It allows our brain to retain an image, albeit for a very short time after we have seen it. The whole illusion of moving pictures depends on this condition." Stuart's attention was hanging on every word.

"The reel of film inside a projector is actually thousands of still pictures strung together on a roll" continued the manager. "The projector shows each picture individually on to the screen but our brain tricks us into thinking they are moving. Do you get it?"

"Er Erm, yes, I think so" answered Stuart looking puzzled.

"Don't worry lad" said the manager "It will all become clearer to you as time goes on." He paused momentarily to think and then made an announcement.

"Okay I'll take you up to the projection room to meet the team. You'll learn more about it all from them".

As they were about to leave the office they heard a feint knocking on the door. A feeble female voice called out.

"Are you in there Mister Thompson?"

The manager smiled and looked at Stuart. "That'll be the *young ladies*. Would you open the door and let them in?"

Stuart sprang to his feet. He naively expected to see some youthful girls. He tugged on a brass handle and the door opened. His anticipated mental picture evaporated. Standing before him were two frail-looking senior ladies! They stared in awe at the young vision before their eyes. They were dressed in identical pale blue cotton smocks. A vertical row of buttons ran from the neck to the knee. The name *Majestic* was embroidered in dark blue cotton above the left breast.

The first lady spoke hesitantly.

"Oh, we were looking for the Manager, Mister Thompson."

The manager stood up and interjected.

"It's all right Mrs. Green I'm here."

Both ladies looked passed Stuart and towards Mister Thompson.

Their wrinkled faces reflected a bewildered expression. The manager spoke again. "Allow me to introduce our new trainee projectionist."

He turned his attention towards Stuart. Holding out the palm of his hand in a cavalier like fashion he said,

"Meet Mrs. Green and her co-worker Mrs. Brown. These are two ladies with colourful names."

He paused for a second. Casting a questioning smile in their direction he added, "And possibly colourful pasts eh ladies?"

The ladies' icy stare melted into an embarrassing smile. They turned their attention again to Stuart. Stopping short of a curtsy they spoke almost in unison.

"Pleased to meet you, I'm sure." Stuart smiled, nodded and returned the compliment. The manager interrupted.

"Did you want me for anything in particular ladies?"

"Ooh, Er, no Mister Thompson we just wanted to make sure you were here. Oh, and we would like to know if we are to do our normal duty tonight?"

Without answering directly the manager asked his own question.

"Have the other ladies arrived yet?"

"Yes Mister Thompson they are in the change room" admitted Mrs. Green.

Taking a sharp breath and then exhaling the manager said "Oh, that's good, thank you ladies. In that case you are both needed in the kiosks. Oh and one more thing.

Would you be kind enough to ask the others to come to my office please; as soon as they can?"

The office door closed. The ladies crossed the foyer like two ducks waddling along a country lane. Mister Thompson turned towards Stuart and spoke.

"Sorry about that lad. Would you sit down again? It might be a good time for you to meet the other staff members. We can go to the projection room later."

The two men sat facing each other as the manager spoke. "Nice ladies don't you think?"

"They both lost their husbands in the Great War and have remained friends ever since."

Stuart nodded in acknowledgement but without feeling obliged to speak.

"Neither of them remarried you know" the manager added.

As Mister Thompson ended his sentence a dark cloud descended over his mood. It caused him to appear to shut down. Like an electric fire when the power is turned off. The glow of the element slowly dims. Stuart had seen his father act in a similar manner. It was when asked about his exploits during the Desert War. His father had been reticent to talk about them. But before Stuart had time to question his mood the manager brightened up again.

"The ladies normally work as cashiers in the kiosks" he said. "They take the money from the patrons. But sometimes if we are short staffed, I help out. I accept the admission money from the people choosing to sit in the balcony."

There was a firm knock on the office door. A loud female voice called out.

"Hello, Mister Thompson, are you there?"

Acting impulsively Stuart stood up.

"Shall I open it sir?" he asked.

The manager nodded.

The door opened and three ladies stood looking inward. They appeared much younger than the previous visitors.

Like their earlier counterparts they also wore pale blue cotton smocks. But each had a singular pocket located near the waistline. All contained a battery-powered torch. They poked from the pockets like a creature peering from a marsupial's pouch.

Closest to the door was a tall lady of medium build. Her long brown hair was worn in a pony tail. In terms of age she was knocking on the door of forty. A second lady stood close behind her. She was shorter in height and enjoying her teenage years.

Blond hair cascaded over her forehead. It had a style reminiscent of an Old English sheepdog. The sides were held back with plastic hair clips. The plastic was fashioned to form the words, *The Beatles.*

Standing in the back ground was a third lady. Her dark eyes peered from beneath a head of equally dark hair. Her face was that of a middle-age woman. It appeared to carry a wealth of experience. There was an air of mystery about her.

Stuart looked at the tall lady. She smiled at him in return. He quickly turned towards the younger one. Instantly he was attracted to her pale blue eyes. They seemed to project a momentary embrace. Then, perhaps overcome by a feeling of shyness, the young lady disengaged. She directed her gaze towards the manager. Stuart looked over her shoulder and took in the image of the third lady. She faced him with penetrating eyes. Her face was expressionless. At that moment the manager spoke out.

"Ladies let me introduce you to Stuart our trainee projectionist."

With the exception of the mysterious one, the ladies looked at him and smiled.

"For the benefit of Stuart" said the manager "here is Janet." He pointed to the lady nearest the door. In like manner he pointed to the younger one.

"And this is Suzie" he announced. "She's a Beatles' fan. Isn't that right Suzie?"

She smiled and nodded whilst flashing a furtive glance at Stuart. He was looking straight at her.

The manager turned his eyes towards the mysterious lady. "Now I must not forget our very important staff member" he said. Tilting his head back slightly and almost pointing with his chin, he spoke.

"Over there is Maureen. She's the lady who keeps the cinema clean and tidy. An absolute wiz with a broom! Oh, and she also sees into the future. She is gifted with second sight. If you ever want to know what your future holds speak to Maureen."

A faint trace of a smile was vaguely discernible on Maureen's face.

Lowering his head again the manager concluded.

"Well ladies, the show will be starting soon, so let's all get back to our jobs shall we?"

As an afterthought he quickly made a suggestion,

"I'm sure you'll be seeing more of Stuart in the future." He turned to face the cleaning lady and spoke again.

"Anyway" he said "Maureen should be able to confirm that. Isn't that so Maureen?"
Realising he was hinting at her gift of clairvoyance everyone chuckled.

CHAPTER TWO

The manager purposely eyed his watch then quickly proclaimed "The second house will be starting soon." Pausing momentarily he looked at Stuart. "But I think there'll be enough time to show you the projection room" he added. Beckoning Stuart to follow him he locked the office door. The two cashiers watched from their kiosks as the men crossed the foyer. A fleeting thought amused Stuart's fertile mind. The cashiers reminded him of passengers in a passing railway carriage.
A mix of people gathered outside the cinema. Turning towards the kiosks the manager called out.
"Hello ladies! I'll open the doors to let the

public in. Then I'll take Stuart to see the projection room!"

The cashiers smiled and nodded.

Stuart followed the manager as he climbed the marble stairway. At the top of the steps Suzie was guarding the balcony entrance. She was armed with a torch and a steel spike having a string attached. The light from the torch would help her guide patrons to their seats. The spike with the string attached would hold the spent portion of their entrance ticket.

"Hello Suzie" said the manager.

"I'm taking Stuart to see the projection room."

Suzie smiled approvingly. She also flashed a look at Stuart. He smiled at her in response. She felt her cheeks begin to blush but in the subdued lighting Stuart didn't notice.

To one side of the balcony entrance was a discreet black painted door. Behind it was a narrow wooden staircase that led to the projection room.

"Follow me Stuart and watch your step" advised the manager. The two plodded up the stairs with their shoulders almost touching the walls on either side. The sound of their shoes on the wooden steps was amplified in the confined space.

Towards the summit they could hear the muffled sound of voices. They stemmed from the sound track of the film that was being shown.

The two men gained the top of the stairs. They entered into an open area that preceded the projection room. The lighting was almost apologetic. A single tungsten globe burned inside a glass protective dome.

"Hello" called out the manager.

A figure suddenly appeared like a Jack-in-the-box in the intervening doorway. It was a tall and lean looking man in his late twenties. He wore a grey long-sleeved shirt and a pink tie. His face was gaunt and his voice sounded strangely effeminate.

Acting as if taken by surprise the man spoke.

"Oh! It's Mister Thompson! Hello. How nice to see you. Are you well?"

The manager responded nonchalantly.

"Hello Clarence. Yes I'm fine thanks. Is Brian there?"

"Yes Mister Thompson, he's right here."

Clarence turned about and pointed towards his colleague. He was standing alongside one of the two projectors.

Brian was a medium sized man in his late forties. He wore a long-sleeved shirt with a brown tie. His form of apparel was considered mandatory for projectionists. The addition of a jacket was expected to be worn when in the public's eye. The black painted projector almost dwarfed him. But his shock of red hair stood out above the top of the machine's lamp house. Speaking with an undefined accent he called out.

"Hello Mister Thompson" he said and moved quickly into full view.

"Gentlemen, could I have a word with you both? " inquired the manager.

Brian and Clarence moved closer together. They stood almost to attention next to the machines. Their faces radiated a look of expectancy. Standing to the one side of Stuart the manager explained.

"This young man is called Stuart. He is your new assistant projectionist. I hope you will give him all the help he needs."

Stuart looked helplessly at the two men. They smiled and nodded in silent affirmation. Clarence's eyes narrowed slightly. They looked at Stuart with particular interest. The manager noticed the look and appeared to stiffen. Solemnly he coughed as if to clear his throat.

"All right then gentlemen" he said "I'll leave Stuart with you. Oh; would you show him how you start the show? I'll come back for him later on."

The men nodded in agreement and the manager turned to leave.

Stuart looked wide eyed around the room. It seemed no bigger than his own bedroom. But the one main difference was the walls. They were painted matt black. It was an attempt to prevent reflected light. The two tall projectors dominated the central floor area. Stuart imagined them to be metallic beasts having arrived from a distant galaxy. "Had they come to take over the world?" he thought.

Both pointed towards small windows that were let into a nearby wall. They faced the auditorium and were aligned with the curtained cinema screen.

Stuart's head moved slowly from left to right. His eyes surveyed the various pieces of apparatus that festooned the walls. There was the steel shutters that hung directly above the small windows. They were designed to fall like guillotines in the event of a fire. The intention being to stop any flames from leaving the projection room and entering into the balcony area.

A solitary recorded disc was pinned to a wall above a record player.

The title of the recording was appropriately named *Blaze Away*. Someone had wisely chosen this particular piece. It was meant to be played in the event of a fire breaking out. The cinema's staff members were trained to evacuate the public if ever they heard its musical refrain.

During the early days of cinema, rolls of film were made from highly flammable material. Under certain conditions it could readily catch alight. The pages of history had recorded a few disastrous incidents.

Fortunately the latest non-flammable film more or less guaranteed the unlikelihood of a fire. But the mechanical precautions remained in place.

Stuart's eyes caught sight of a black metal box that dominated the centre of a wall. It was the sound amplifier that accepted audio from the projectors. Once amplified the sound could be conveyed to the cinema's loudspeakers. Continuing their journey of exploration Stuart's eyes stopped abruptly. It was as if they had reached the end of a dark chasm. In a sense they had. They were looking directly into the face of Clarence.

The tall gaunt figure stood silently analyzing Stuart's every move. His blond hair was parted on the left side and sat neatly above his forehead. Although his face was recently shaved some tufts of stubble remained. They looked like hardy weeds sprouting from a newly mown lawn. As he spoke globules of spittle formed in the corners of his mouth. His lips stretched to form a suppressed smile.

"Hello Stuart" he began. "How old are you buddy?"

Responding to this unexpected question Stuart proudly answered.

"I'm fifteen going on sixteen."

Clarence simply smiled whilst displaying a peculiar glint in his eyes.

"What do you think of the manager then?"

He asked somewhat slyly.

Stuart answered cautiously.

"Well, I think he is a really nice person and a genuine sort of bloke. He's very helpful and an interesting man to listen to. In short I'd call him a realist."

Stuart had heard the expression 'A realist' some time before. He liked to use new words when the situation allowed.

Clarence felt inwardly impressed. It seemed to him that the boy had integrity. But then he wondered. Was he just pulling the proverbial wool over his eyes? He thought he would test him with another question.

"Did he tell you about his wife?" he continued.

"Er no he didn't" answered Stuart. "Why is he married?"

"Well he *was*" said Clarence and then quickly added the word, "*Briefly!*" He emphasised the two words 'was' and 'briefly.'

"Oh yes" said Stuart remembering, "I did see a wedding photograph inside his office desk. I suppose that must have been one of him and his wife. But what do you mean 'Briefly?' "

Clarence glanced nervously towards Brian. Throughout the conversation he had stood quietly to one side. Immediately afterwards, Clarence looked into the adjacent room. He made sure no one was there and especially Mister Thompson. Before speaking again he seemed to writhe slightly. He acted like a snake moving into a striking position.

"Well buddy," he began. "During the war years Mister Thompson met up with a young woman. They hadn't known each other long before they decided to get wed. Living was a risky business in those days. Decisions had to be made quickly. You were never too sure if one of Hitler's bombs was going to get you." Remembering that Brian had encountered bombs during his military

career, he cast him a questioning look. Since there was no response he continued. "After the wedding ceremony, there was a bit of a 'do' at the local Co-operative Halls."
Brian interrupted for the first time.
"I believe that's the place where *The Beatles* are going to visit!" he exclaimed.
Clarence looked quizzical when Brian spoke. He had heard of *The Beatles* but couldn't bring them to mind. A few moments later he remembered.
"Of course; *The Beatles!* The new music group from Liverpool. I hear they're coming to our town. It's my guess they're going to be famous. "
Clarence spoke louder as he attempted to override the interruption.
"Anyway; to continue. The newlyweds went to Blackpool for their honeymoon. They booked into a posh boarding house for a few days. Then, on their wedding night...."
Clarence stopped abruptly. He looked at Brian as though he wanted his consent before continuing. Brian offered a look of silent approval. Clarence continued.
"I suppose you could say they had a bit of rumpty-tumpty and a bit of how's your father?"
Stuart looked puzzled. Clarence noticed his

expression and was inwardly amused by Stuart's apparent naivety. He slowly puckered his lips and clenched his fist. Then he made a lateral thrusting motion with his arm. Pushing back and forth he pretended it was a penis.

"Well you know what I mean?" he said.

Clarence added some emphasis to his following sentence. "Anyway! " he began.

"The next morning when Mister Thompson wakes up, all luvy duvy like, he turned to Mrs Thompson to say "Good morning". Maybe he gave her a little nudge, having one thing on his mind like."

Clarence looked at Brian and raised his eyebrows expecting a response.

Wishing to avoid eye contact Brian quickly looked down at the floor.

Appearing unperturbed Clarence returned his attention to Stuart.

"Then he notices she is cold like. So he says softly "Hey luvy are you warm enough?" But she doesn't answer. So he starts to rub her back; gentle like. But then he thinks, hang on a minute her whole body is cold. That can't be right. He speaks a lot louder and shakes her a bit. Nothing happens."

At this moment Stuart was totally captivated by Clarence's words. He also felt tears pricking his eyes.

"Then he raises his voice and shakes her proper like" continued Clarence. "But still there's no response! It suddenly dawns on him something is very wrong. He gets out of bed and goes around to her side. He has a good look at her. Finally; he realises she is not breathing. She's dead! What a shock for the poor beggar."

Brian looked downcast.

Stuart surreptitiously raised a hand. With a fore-finger he brushed away a tear from his eye. Clarence quickly noted his audience's reaction. His face morphed into a look of evil satisfaction. His mouth developed a sordid smirk. To top all of this he couldn't resist the temptation to add a little levity to his tale. As he spoke globules of spittle formed again in the corners of his mouth. They stretched like pieces of chewing gum as his lips opened and closed.

"I suppose" he said "that on the wedding night he got on top of her like, if you know what I mean? You know, to perform his duty like. Then I suppose you might say like, when he was cumin' she was goin'!"

Clarence cackled like a demented jack ass. Droplets of spittle left the corners of his mouth and flew through the air. Brian and

Stuart stared blankly.

Although realising the intended humour in the words, they were mortified out of respect for their manager. Clarence was enjoying his little quip but gradually realised his listeners were not amused. He slowly restrained himself and spoke in a mildly apologetic way.

"Well just to finish my tale" he said sheepishly "It wasn't long afterwards when Mister Thompson enlisted in the army."

Responding to Clarence's change of mood his audience looked at him again.

"He was posted to North Africa like. I suppose he saw enough there to take his mind off things."

The sound of a banging door brought the talk to an abrupt end. All three men stood silent and listened. A second later a female voice was heard to call out.

"Hello! Is anyone there?"

Footsteps could be heard. They plodded up the wooden stairs from the floor below. Brian moved towards the projection room doorway. He looked into the adjoining room. The tall figure of an usherette walked towards him. The beam from her torch bathed the floor boards with extra light.

"It's Janet" announced Brian.

The others looked on in anticipation of her entrance. Brian stepped back out of her way.

"Hello gentlemen" said Janet as she stood in the doorway. "Mister Thompson has sent me up. He says you can start the show when you're ready. He says to tell you it's almost seven o'clock and he knows how forgetful you both are."

Both men looked shocked. A second later the expression on Clarence's face turned to one of indignation.

"The cheeky beggar!" he exclaimed. "He's the one who is forgetful; and usually when it comes to paying us our wages!"

"Yes, that's right" agreed Brian laughingly.

Janet quickly focused her eyes on Stuart.

"Oh, yes" she said "And Mister Thompson said he's sorry he couldn't come up for you but he would like to see you in his office before home time."

The expressions on the faces of Clarence and Brian changed to one of surprise.

"Ooh; I say; I wonder what he wants?" blurted Clarence.

"It's none of your business" retorted Janet. She had known Clarence for some time and wasn't overly fond of him. When she spoke to him it was always quick and to the point.

Turning her attention once more towards Stuart she asked a question.

"When are you on duty again luv?"

Stuart tried to remember.

"Er Saturday afternoon, for the matinee, I think. But I'll have to make sure with Mister Thompson first."

"Okay" said Janet. "So I'll see you on Saturday. The ladies will have a little surprise for you."

Clarence and Brian looked at each other and raised their eyebrows.

Janet called out "See you later gentlemen."

She almost sang her words as she made her way towards the stairs.

Stuart turned to face his colleagues who were eyeing him intently.

"I wonder what surprise she has for me?"
he asked.

"Search me luv" said Clarence sarcastically.

"You'll have to wait for Saturday to find out won't you now?"

Brian retracted a shirt cuff to expose his watch.

"Wow!" he exclaimed "It's three minutes to seven. We'd better start the show."

"Right" spouted Clarence. He turned and called to Stuart.

"You can watch us working buddy but don't get under our feet!"

The two men took up their positions. Each stood next to his own projector. Brian checked the time again. He reached out to a rheostat secured to a wall. His fingers eased its sliding lever slowly towards the floor. Without letting it go he stretched forward to peer through a small glass window. He could see the huge auditorium lights grow dimmer as he continued to slide the lever. At the same time the shafts of light below the screen's curtains grew shorter.

Clarence stood next to his projector having pushed a button to activate its lamp house. A huge xenon lamp was glowing brightly inside. His hand was poised on an electrical switch. At precisely seven o'clock he activated the drive motor. The projector began to rumble and transport the film. He pulled a lever on the lamp house releasing the light from its source. Flickering images of numbers shone on the blinkered window in front of the machine. The numbers counted down from ten to one. They were followed by the image of a *Certificate of Approval.*

Every film was awarded a Certificate of Approval by the British Board of Film

Censors. The official body vetted every film before it was seen by the public. If it was considered to be too violent or too sexual it could be banned.

Clarence operated a second lever. It lifted the steel shutter that covered the window. The certificate's image was released. It shone through the window and into the auditorium. By flicking a switch Clarence allowed the audio, from the film's soundtrack, to be heard through the cinema's loud speakers. Simultaneously Brian pressed an electrical button causing the huge curtains to open. The beam of light from Clarence's projector travelled through the air and across the length of the auditorium.

Dust motes twinkled like glitter seemingly suspended in its wake. In an instant it reached the screen and filled it with moving images. The light reflected from the screen and on to the numerous faces of the viewing audience. Various people smoked cigarettes whilst here and there a pipe or two were evident. The resultant smoke rose lazily towards the ceiling. On its journey it became visible as it passed through the light beam. Swirling and forming shapes it caused the light to have a bluish hue. Fortunately it made no difference to the moving pictures on the screen.

Clarence made a final gesture. Opening a small window in the nearby wall he placed his ear next to it. He listened to the audio stemming from the cinema's loudspeakers.

Sometimes it was necessary to make a small adjustment to the volume. As it happened all systems were running smoothly. The reel of film was expected to run for twenty minutes before the next one was required. Clarence turned to Stuart and asked a question.

"So what did you think about that buddy?"

"Well it seemed pretty exciting" said Stuart "But what happens when the reel of film runs out?"

"That's when we do a change-over" said Clarence.

Stuart looked puzzled again.

"A change-over" he pondered "What's a change-over?"

Clarence chuckled.

"That's when we switch-on the other machine" he said. He saw Stuart's puzzled expression and realised more explanation was needed.

"All right then, let me tell you. The whole show runs for two hours. Usually one reel of film runs for twenty minutes. So for two hours that would mean six reels of film. Do you agree?"

Clarence raised an eyebrow and cocked his head on one side. He looked at Stuart expecting a reply. Stuart juggled the figures inside his head. He didn't fully
 understanding.

"Did you say the show runs for two hours?" he asked.

"That's right" said Clarence heaving a sigh. "Two hours or one hundred and twenty minutes if you like" he added, making his point as clear as possible.

"So that means if one reel of film runs for twenty minutes, then one hundred and twenty, divided by twenty, equals six. Get it?"

Stuart's face was contorted.

"I think I sort of 'get it" said Stuart "but what about the change-over?"

"Ah yes - the change-over" said Clarence.

Sensing that he was making some progress Clarence replied "Well, I'll tell you. The six reels of film are shared between the two projectors. They are shown alternately between the two machines. Do you follow?" Stuart nodded silently.

"We run the first reel of film on the number

one projector. Then when it finishes we run the second reel of film on the number two projector. Do you understand?" asked Clarence.

"Erm, yes. I think I'm starting to understand" answered Stuart more confidently.

Clarence continued.

"Once the first reel of film has finished we do a change-over. And that is when we switch on the second projector to show the second reel of film. So we have changed over from one projector to the other. Do you see now?"

Stuart's face suddenly relaxed.

"Ah yes" he said "I think the penny has finally dropped!"

"Good!" exclaimed Clarence heaving a sigh of relief.

He looked at his wristwatch.

"Look" he said "We've got about fifteen minutes before we switch on the other machine. But right now I've got to go down stairs. When I come back I'll show you what we do. Okay? "

"Yes that's fine thanks" answered Stuart.

Brian was sitting on a wooden stool next to his projector. Clarence called out to him. His voice could barely be heard above the sounds of the projector and the film's soundtrack.

"Hey Brian" he shouted "I'm going down stairs for a few minutes. I'll be back for the change over!"

Brian responded with a thumb up sign showing that he understood. Clarence returned a sly smile and turned about. He disappeared through the open doorway.

CHAPTER THREE

As Clarence left the room Brian stood up. He walked over to the active projector to check that the film was running smoothly. Satisfied that all was well he called to Stuart.

"So Stuart what do you do when you are not here? I mean to say do you have a full time job?"

"Yes I have" answered Stuart "I'm an electrical apprentice."

"Oh, how shocking!" quipped Brian.

They both chuckled.

Stuart formed the impression that Brian was quite different to Clarence. He sensed that he meant him no harm.

"What kind of electrical work do you do?" asked Brian, his face displaying an encouraging smile.

Stuart appeared thoughtful.

"I work for an electrical contracting company. We do a lot of work on building sites. We install lights and power to newly built premises."

"Sounds like hard work" suggested Brian.

"Yes I suppose it is" said Stuart "But there are times when we have some laughs."

"Oh yes?" responded Brian as he raised his eyebrows in anticipation of a follow up story.

"Well" continued Stuart, remembering an incident. "There was one site I worked on where a tall office block was to be built. A deep oblong trench had been dug to put down the foundations. It was around four feet deep and many square feet in area."

Stuart stopped to think for a few seconds. He mentally arranged the facts of the story in their right order.

"The construction workers drove Dumpster trucks" Stuart recalled. "They used them to move the loose soil from one place to another. They were strange looking contraptions and powered by a noisy diesel engine."

Stuart added "The engine was situated behind the driver's seat. The truck was low on speed but high on torque. And at the front was a huge bucket-like container which carried the soil."

Brian suddenly interrupted.

"Just let me check that the projector is running smoothly" he said. After a quick look at the picture on the cinema screen and a listen to the film's audio he was satisfied that all was well. He gave Stuart the go ahead.

"As I was saying" continued Stuart "The odd thing about the Dumpster truck was that the steering wheel operated the rear wheels. By contrast the front wheels were locked in the forward position. I later found this to be quite a problem."

Brian looked surprised.

"Are you old enough to drive?" he asked quizzically.

"No I'm not" admitted Stuart "But I am taking unofficial driving lessons. I drive anything whenever I get the chance!"

They both smiled.

Stuart continued with his story.

"My foreman knew I was 'learning' to drive.

He had also seen me looking at the Dumpsters with envious eyes. One day he told me in no uncertain terms not to go anywhere near them. Well, that was like asking a bird not to fly!"

Brian chuckled.

"So what did you do next?" he asked excitedly.

"Well, I watched and waited for my moment to arrive. I saw that every lunch break a certain driver would park his Dumpster near to the trench. He would then join the other site workers in their cabin. The trades' people shared a different one. It so happened that the driver would let the Dumpster's engine tick over. This was because it was such an effort to start.

It required swinging on a steel cranking handle to get the engine to run."

Stuart took a deep breath.

"My red letter day eventually arrived. The siren for the lunch break sounded. All the workers scurried to their hut like bees to a hive. I followed my co-workers to our cabin. On the way I noticed the Dumpster had been left near the trench in the usual manner. The engine was barely running with the tick over speed so low. My moment of glory was about to arrive. Everyone in our cabin was engrossed in talking and eating. I managed to slip out without drawing too much attention. The coast was clear. No one was in sight. There was just me and the Dumpster. And of course the trench; which lay some twenty feet to the front of me."

Brian was smiling broadly. He was enjoying the story.

"So what happened then?" he asked impatiently.

"A quick glance around, to make sure no one was about and I climbed into the driver's seat" admitted Stuart. "I recognised the layout. It was similar to a car that I was familiar with. Of course the Dumpster had fewer comforts. Naturally the steering wheel was there. It was a huge steel thing.

So too was three plain steel pedals. They comprised the clutch, the brake and the accelerator. Next to the driver's seat was a long bent steel rod. It was the gear's stick that operated the gear box."

"Anxiously with my left foot I pushed down hard on the clutch pedal. Next I pushed the long gear stick away from me. It willingly selected the first gear. The Dumpster gave a small lurch forward. I remembered to release the primitive hand brake. Slowly I eased the pressure off the clutch pedal.

The Dumpster was trying to move forward without help from me. My right foot lightly touched the accelerator pedal. The noise from the engine grew louder. Chug, chug, chug, chug, was the sound it made."

"The Dumpster lurched forward again and its speed seemed to increase unaided by my effort. I turned the steering wheel. The Dumpster travelled in opposition to my desire. I could see the distance between the trench and myself getting shorter. What made matters worse was a thick layer of mud that lay on the ground. It was the result of recent heavy rains. The steel monster moved steadily forward.

Chug, chug, chug, chug, was the sound its engine made. I battled frantically with the steering wheel to change direction.

But the Dumpster had its own idea. It simply wanted to travel straight on."

"Within three feet of the trench I had finally figured out how to steer. But alas it was too late! I managed to jump off as the mechanical beast nosedived into the trench! I landed knees first into a heap of mud. After picking myself up I stood with mud covering my shoes. My gaze fell on to the smoking tail end of the Dumpster. It poked skyward from the trench like the stern end of a sinking ship. Miraculously though it seemed, the engine continued to tick over. Gradually, the noise of the chugging engine was drowned by the sounds of jeering and howling. They came from the building site workforce. The men had turned out of their huts en mass to look."

Brian was in fits of laughter. Stuart simply stood and coolly smiled. He had told the story many times before. He waited until Brian's laughter had petered out. Then he asked him a question.

"So Brian, what did you do before you worked at the cinema?" Brian composed himself. His face took on a serious expression.

"So it's my turn now is it?" he asked. He spent a few seconds in thought. "All right" he said, as though he was ready to begin.

"Well, going back a bit in time I was in the army during the war years. I was with the first Battalion of the 'Loyals'. Actually they were called 'The Loyal Regiment, North Lancashire'.

We were based at Preston barracks to start with."

"So what did you do whilst with them?" asked Stuart.

"I was with a bomb disposal squad."

"Really?" exclaimed Stuart. "That must have been dangerous?"

Without trying to feign any false modesty Brian shot his answer straight from the hip.

"Yes it was! We had one or two fatalities. They were due to bombs being fitted with an additional fuse."

"What do you mean when you say an additional fuse?" asked Stuart.

Brian's face took on a look of deep concentration. His facial expression changed from moment to moment. It showed pain and surprise and then sorrow and joy. Silently, within the confines of his mind he was reliving some of his war time experiences. A few moments later his facial expression froze. It seemed to suggest he had now reached an understanding of what he was about to say.

"Well first of all" Brian began, "I was in North Africa, at a place called Bir Hacheim. Enemy aeroplanes were bombing the coastal road with the intention of making it impassable. The road was essential for our trucks to carry supplies to our troops. At Bir Hacheim a few bombs had been dropped. One or two had landed on the road and had failed to explode. Our squad was called in."

Stuart interrupted. "Which squad was that?"

"Oh sorry" said Brian "I should have said the bomb disposal unit."

"We worked in pairs and had a telephone with which to speak to our officers. They of course were some distance from us and out of sight. The idea was that one of us would work on the bomb whilst the other spoke into the telephone."

"Why would you need to speak into a telephone?" Stuart queried.

"Well during the course of de-fusing any bomb, all our movements were spoken into a telephone. That way if something should go wrong, then at least the officers would know what our last movement had been."

Stuart silently nodded to show that he understood.

"On one occasion" said Brian "Two of the lads were busy doing their job. They were working on a large bomb that lay on its side. Its fuse was about a foot from the nose end. Each move they made was dutifully relayed by telephone to their superiors. Sand was packed around the bomb to stop it from moving. The screws holding the fuse into position had been removed." Brian coughed to clear his throat.

"The fuse was carefully lifted from the body of the bomb casing." Stuart watched Brian's hands as they appeared to be miming the actions of the bomb disposal man.

"Some wires were attached to its underside. One by one the wires were cut with a tool.

All was going well. The soldier announced his next move. He was about to lift the fuse away from the bomb. No sooner had the telephonist relayed the words when there was an incredible explosion!"

Brian ceased talking. Thoughts ran riot inside his head. He remained silent. He was in a state of suspended animation. It lasted for a few seconds. Eventually he spoke but with a faltering voice.

"All that remained was a crater. It was twelve feet in diameter and four feet deep!"

Stuart stared in wonderment. There was a pregnant pause in conversation. It was as if both parties were drawing on reserves of energy. Brian secretly raised a finger to blot a tear that had formed under his eye.

In due course Stuart broke the silence by hesitantly asking a question.

"Did you say there were a *couple* of fatalities?"

"Yes that's right" said Brian. "When working on the second bomb it was noticed that there was something extra attached to the fuse. But soon after the telephonist gave a description, the bomb exploded. The end result was the same as the first." Brian took a deep breath. "Then," he declared "it came my turn to tackle a similar bomb".

Brian was trying hard to control his emotions. He reached into his trouser pocket and pulled out a packet of Polo mints. He popped one into his mouth and offered the packet to Stuart. Brian sucked on the mint and continued with his story.

"I had listened to all the information and memorised what had been said. Now I was in the lion's den."

Stuart allowed his curiosity to overcome his discretion. "Weren't you scared?" he asked.

Brian looked away, trying not to betray his feelings. His tongue pushed the mint to one side of his mouth as he answered.

"An officer must show no particular emotion" he said "But I would be lying if I said I wasn't scared."

He turned his head slowly and looked directly at Stuart.

"Somehow" he admitted "I used my fear as a tool to work with me. I actually used it to defeat my fear!"

He gestured towards the floor.

"I found myself kneeling next to the bomb. I considered it to be my protagonist.

It lay there silent and inanimate. It appeared as a huge metallic mass that had no life. And yet, to me it had a spiritual energy. It was an energy that was testing me."

Brian pondered his words for a while. "Yes" he said, as though he had arrived at an answer to a self asking question. "It was a contest between *it* and *me.*

Or perhaps it was a testing of two spiritual energies."

Brian looked at Stuart and wondered if he understood what he was saying. Stuart appeared to be awe struck.

Brian continued.

"I went through the necessary motions. The telephonist relayed my instructions faithfully to the distant onlookers. Then I reached the part when the wires had been cut. They were the ones that connected the fuse to the bomb. I knelt on the ground poised. One hand steadied me against the body of the metallic predator. My free hand was holding the fuse. I remembered it being mentioned that something extra was attached to it. Carefully; oh so very carefully, I lowered my head. As my eyes re-focused, incredibly I could see a thin piece of material attached to the fuse. It went on into the innards of the bomb. It was almost invisible next to the wires. But once the wires were out of the way it could be seen. My hand was getting tired and the fuse was becoming heavier. No one was able to help me. I had to make my own decision.

Curiously it entered my head to cut the strip of material in much the same way that I had cut the wires. Whilst still holding the fuse I reached with my other hand for the cutters. At the point when the cutters were about to work, my hand began to tremble. Fortunately, as it was, one snip and the material was cut. Nothing happened! The fuse was separated from the bomb. The contest was over. I was the winner!"

Stuart had been hanging on every word. He could hardly contain himself as he asked another question.

"So what was that material thing you cut? What was it there for?"

Brian had clearly been re-living the event he had described. Now he spoke with less emotion.

"It turned out" he said "that the material was designed to trigger a detonator. It was located at the front end of the bomb."

Brian slowed the pace of his words.

"If the fuse failed to do its job in the normal way" he said "then when the material was pulled it would achieve the same result!"

The two projectionists had been so engrossed in their conversation that they had failed to notice the moving film's progress. Brian's mind left the sands of the Western Desert. He glanced at the projector's top spool box. "Blimey!" he cried "The reel is almost empty. "

Sounding annoyed he added "Clarence should have been back before now!"

Stuart was filled with fear. He looked on in silence.

"Never mind" uttered Brian "I'll do the change over myself."

"Can I do anything to help?" called Stuart.

"It's Okay. Just keep to one side and watch." With seconds to spare Brian dashed to the standby projector. He flicked an electric switch on the lamp house. It caused the xenon lamp to burst into life.

Quickly lowering his head he peered through a small glass window. He viewed the images presently showing on the cinema screen. His trained eye watched and waited for a small black dot to appear. Suddenly it was there; at the top right corner of the screen. But only for a fraction of a second. It was Brian's cue to switch on the electric motor.

The projector sprang to life. He pulled a lever on the lamp house. A narrow horizontal shaft of light fell onto the moving film. Brian continued to watch the screen. He waited for a second black dot to appear. Seconds later it happened. With one hand he flicked a switch. The audio from the second projector was instantly diverted to the auditorium.

His free hand pushed down on the lever attached to the guillotine arrangement. A steel shutter in front of his projector's lens was lifted. The film's moving image shot across the auditorium and hit the big screen. Simultaneously a steel shutter fell in front of the first projector's lens and blocked its light.

The brief switch of images from one machine to the other went unnoticed by the audience. Stuart had watched in amazement as the process took less than three minutes. The film passed smoothly through the projector. The magical, moving images of light, flickered on the screen. The continuity of the film's story had been preserved. Brian called out triumphantly.

"That's it, another successful change over!"

At that moment Clarence stormed into the room. He stood looking slightly dishevelled and distinctly careworn. His voice sounded breathless.

"Hello buddies I'm back! Sorry for the delay. I got held up! Is everything all right?"

The two men looked at each other. Stuart's face erupted into a smile. Brian raised his eyebrows in exasperation. He slowly exhaled as he answered

"Yes Clarence, everything is fine."

CHAPTER FOUR

Clarence looked apologetically at his two work mates. "Is there anything I can do to help you buddies?" he asked.

"Yes there is" said Brian sternly. "If you like, you can take the used reel of film off number one projector and re-wind it."

"Okay" said Clarence. He moved eagerly towards the machine. Opening the door of the bottom spool box he looked inside. It contained a reel holding two thousand feet of transported film. He remembered that it had taken twenty minutes for the film to travel through the projector. Suddenly it occurred to him that's how long he had been away! A feeling of guilt crept into his mind. By way of seeking redemption he turned to Brian. "Shall I load the next reel of film on to the projector?" he asked.

Brian agreed. Clarence took the spent reel to the annexe of the projection room. He placed it onto the rewinding machine and grabbed the next reel from a storage rack. Returning to the projector he began to lace the film through the machine. Stuart spoke out. His curiosity had got the better of him.

He reminded Brian of their interrupted conversation.

"So what did you do when the war ended?" asked Stuart.

"Ah yes" said Brian, remembering where he had left off. "About a year or so after the end of the war, the Government introduced a scheme. It was an idea to create much needed jobs for the ex-service men. They would be required to travel to Africa. To the country that was then called Tanganyika.

The idea was to cultivate ground nuts."

Stuart's face looked perplexed.

"What are ground nuts?" he asked.

As Clarence threaded the film around the projector's various sprockets he casually listened to the conversation. But when he heard Stuart's question he paused and waited intently for Brian's answer.

"Well" began Brian "ground nuts are actually climbing vines that produce bulb-like tubers from the root system. The tubers are what we know as peanuts. Although some varieties can grow as big as an apple. The tubers can be processed to produce vegetable oil that is used for cooking. Because of the World War there was a general shortage of it. The project was intended to grow the nuts on a grand scale." Stuart smiled indicating that he understood. Clarence listened with growing interest.

"The Government" continued Brian, "advertised the project which was mainly aimed at ex-soldiers. Surprisingly in a short time a few thousand blokes applied for the jobs. Collectively they were known as the 'Groundnut Army'. As it turned out me and my pal were two of them."

As Clarence heard the confession he instantly saw an opportunity to call out a jibe. "I'll bet they had a real pair of *nuts* when you two joined them!" he chortled.

Brian looked at Stuart. They tried to remain serious but failed. The three projectionists laughed out loud. A minute or two later the laughter ceased. Clarence resumed his work and Brian continued with his story.

"They sent us to Africa in an old cargo ship" Brian recalled. "When we arrived there we encountered all manner of wild things. There were lions, crocodiles, elephants and rhinoceros, to name but a few. I remember one day I was with some of the blokes. We were sitting around a makeshift table placed next to some trees. The afternoon sun was low in the sky. We were chatting and drinking beers. At that time of day a drink of ice-chilled beer is known as a 'sun-downer'. Just as we were about to start our third drink, or sun downer, there was a loud noise. It came from a group of nearby huts. It sounded like a runaway express train. We looked up and saw huts sent flying. Some were crushed into splinters. The local men, women and children rushed around aimlessly in terrified helplessness. There was a hippopotamus running amuck. It appeared to be heading straight for us. We all just froze. It was as if we were mesmerised. But luckily an officer saw what was happening. He came running up holding a revolver he had drawn from its holster. He stood facing the animal as bold as brass. We thought perhaps he was going to shoot it but not so. Instead he stood cool as a cucumber and waited until the animal was a few feet away. Then he fired three shots into the air. The hippo immediately slowed down. It seemed startled by the sound."

Brian stared wide eyed as he looked at Stuart.

"Do you know, I could swear it looked the officer in his eyes! The moment of truth had arrived. We expected the animal to attack. But imagine our surprise and utmost relief when the unwanted visitor moved off into the bush!"

Clarence had finished his task. He was staring at Brian with an incredulous look. Stuart's head was shaking slowly from side to side. He was visually expressing his amazement. Before either of them could make a further comment Brian pressed on with his tale.

"But perhaps the most aggressive and yet smallest danger we faced was bees."

After listening to Brian's latest statement Clarence recognised another chance for a jibe. He couldn't restrain himself. This time he made a "Buzz a buzz, buzz a buzz" sound. Brian was not amused.

"Oh do be quiet!" he said "I'm trying to finish this story."

Clarence grimaced momentarily and then quickly responded.

"Okay" he replied "I'll bee (sic) good and I'll buzz off!"

Chuckling to himself he walked into the annexe. He began rewinding the used reel of film. Brian heaved a small sigh of relief as he watched him leave.

"When we came to move some baobab trees" he continued "We disturbed some bees' nests that were living inside. Lots of the lads were badly stung. My pal was one of them. He was taken to hospital for treatment."

"Were you stung?" inquired Stuart.

"No, I was one of the fortunate ones. For some obscure reason the bees avoided me. My pal soon recovered and sometime later we attended an interview with some army officers."

"The meeting took place in what looked like an old wooden shack. I remember it even had a thatch roof. But as we entered we were surprised to find that it served as the local pub. At a table facing us sat two decorated officers. We approached them across a wooden floor. Dust rose to form clouds through which the sunlight pierced. Round about us were seated various personnel. All were quaffing quantities of beer. Some of them were smoking a local brand of cigarette. They formed a chorus of coughers who we heard above the sound of garrulous voices."

"One of the officers looked at me through the bottom of an upraised glass. His hair was white and it appeared as if bleached by the sun. It was parted exactly in the middle of his head. The parted halves were neatly trimmed and brushed back. His sun-tanned face had a crumpled look about it. He slurred his words as he lowered his glass.

"What will you have to drink old chap?"

"As he spoke the sun was sitting low on the distant horizon. Its rays shone through an open window. They reflected off the brass pips attached to the epaulettes of his bush jacket. Above a breast pocket he wore three medal ribbons. They had been awarded for his service during the First World War. My pal and I accepted the offer and drank a cool refreshing beer.

The second officer spoke next. He wore an extra pip on each epaulette and sported an extra medal ribbon over his breast pocket. "

"Now then chaps, this is what we would like you to do" said the officer. He spoke in a similar way to our present Queen. I don't mean in an effeminate way but rather in a refined way. He said

"We want you to drive one of our Bedford trucks. You will take some of the chaps a few miles north of here to develop a farm."

"Well" explained Brian "We were dumbfounded. But naturally I had to ask the obvious question. "What are we going to do when we get there, sir?" He seemed to pre-empt my question.

"Yes, yes, of course, I shall tell you" retorted the officer. He struggled to swallow another mouthful of beer. As he spoke a drop or two left his mouth. They flew uncontrollably through the air and glinted in the sun's rays.

"You will drive the truck one hundred miles directly north west from here" he explained. "There you will find all the equipment and facilities you may need in order to create a groundnut farm."

The officer carefully placed his glass onto the table. He moved his hand a short distance towards a cardboard folder. After thumbing it open he took from it a sheet of printed paper.

"Here is a contract" he said. "You will each be paid fifty pounds per week to pay for your private needs such as food and drink. Kindly sign on the bottom line and you may see our Quartermaster."

When he said fifty pounds my pal and I nearly fainted. That was a major amount of money in those days. Later on we worked it out that we could live more than adequately on one income and bank the rest.

After the initial shock had subsided I asked the officer how big the farm was. He said it was around a hundred and fifty acres."

"How big is that?" inquired Stuart excitedly.

Brian thought for a moment or two.

"I believe it's almost eighty times bigger than the football ground at London's Wembley Stadium."

"Wow! That's huge!" exclaimed Stuart.

"Yes it is" admitted Brian "But sadly we never saw it!"

"What?...never saw it.......but why?" spluttered Stuart.

"Well later that week a few of us were given an old Bedford truck and told to drive north to the farm site. We were given some supplies and directions and off we went.

After a couple of days of driving, the journey took a turn for the worse. Suddenly a small hole appeared in the front of the windscreen. Then there was another. Bits of glass hit us in the face. We were unsure what was happening. This was followed by audible thuds on the side of the truck. Finally, we realised we were being attacked.

A bullet actually flew through the cab. It turned out we had been sent into a war zone. Well, enough was enough. We hastily turned around and headed straight back to our starting point.

Of course when we got back to head quarters questions were asked. The officers were none too pleased. We argued that we hadn't been told a war was being waged near the farm. At that moment we decided we had had enough. We resigned there and then. Naturally our action was frowned upon. But we were adamant and demanded to be returned to blighty. Eventually everyone saw reason. We planned to purchase a berth on the next cargo ship sailing for home. But we were told to use our own money to pay for the tickets. Thankfully, there was an assurance that we would be refunded in England. So that was it. We had to suffer three and a half more weeks on a tramp steamer on a return journey." .

Brian finished talking and quickly turned his attention to the projector. He glanced through a small glass window in the top spool box. He could see the reel of film turning smoothly. There was enough film remaining for time to spare before the next change-over. Clarence had listened to Brian's story discretely from the nearby annexe. He had rewound the reel of film some time before. But now he was having difficulty in containing his curiosity. Sensing there was a lull in the conversation he wandered into the projection room. Giving Stuart a look, as if to ask for permission to interrupt, he turned to face Brian.

"Well Brian that was quite an adventure you had."

Brian looked surprised to see Clarence standing near him. But he quickly responded to the remark.

"Yes it was. All part of life's sweet pageant I suppose."

"Oh yeah!" exclaimed Clarence. "All part of life is it? That's all very well but how about death? What do you have to say about death Mister Trent?"

Brian was taken aback by hearing his surname. He was equally stunned by the seemingly profound question. He knew Clarence used his surname whenever he had something important to say. But he hadn't considered him to be a deep thinker.

"Are you serious?" asked Brian.

Clarence's face stiffened and frowned.

"Yes" he said, nodding his head assuredly. Then he thought about his answer for a second. He wanted to be sure that he actually did mean it.

"Yeah, I am serious" he asserted.

"I mean to say, you've seen a lot, done a lot and lived a lot. So let's have your take on the death angle."

Brian looked at the floor for a few moments. He prepared himself mentally for the challenge. Slowly looking up he saw Stuart staring at him. Without saying a word he shifted his gaze towards Clarence. Both men eagerly awaited an answer.

Brian spoke. "I think it was a Jewish writer who wrote that we have two deaths."

There was an instant look of surprise on the listeners' face.

"That's right. We die twice. Once when our body dies. Then again when the memory of our existence dies. At that point we become just a name. Or maybe like a book on a shelf that nobody bothers to read."

Brian looked directly at Stuart.

"Put another way it might be said that for a limited time we are contributing to the world. But once we are dead someone else takes over the role."

Clarence was deep in thought. But the instant Brian stopped Clarence commented.

"A book on a bookshelf you said. Now there's an idea. If I were a book, a very interesting story I could tell, that's for sure!"

"Yes Clarence, I'm convinced of that!" admitted Brian.

Stuart had listened quietly to the conversation but now he felt it was his turn to speak. "But Brian what did you mean when you said we are "Contributing to the world and then someone else takes over the role"?"

"Ah yes" acknowledged Brian "That's a very good question. I'll try my best to answer it."

He fell silent for a time as he mulled things over in his mind.

"Well; it's like this. I like to compare my life to nature. Take for example, a tree. An oak tree or whatever tree you wish. The oak is a classic example since it grows tall and sturdy and is not easily destroyed. But a tree, like any other living thing, has got a finite life span." Brian glanced again at the spool box. There was still plenty of film on the reel.

"Let me take the weight off my feet" he said. He sat on a wooden milking-stool next to the machine.

"That feels better" Brian declared. "One day" he continued "I went for a walk to a place where I do some fishing. It's a secluded spot near an old factory. At the site is a large catchment area. You might even call it a medium size lake. Spring water flows into it at one end. Whilst at the other end the overflow creates a rivulet. One side of the lake is overshadowed by a clump of oak trees. They were deliberately planted to screen the view of the factory from some nearby houses. The trees must have been planted some years ago since they are a considerable height." Brian paused to look at his watch. "Anyway" he said "my fishing line was cast on the water and all was well. Nearby birds were making their twittering sounds. The occasional rumble of a bus or a truck could be heard in the distance. But in general all was peaceful. But all of a sudden and without invitation a loud cracking sound began. It disrupted the tranquillity of the scene. I looked up and saw a couple of young boys. They were busy breaking branches from a nearby tree. In view of what I've already said you can perhaps imagine my state of mind. My immediate reaction was to call out to the boys.

"Hey, you boys, what are you doing?"

Of course this was a rhetorical question. The boys and I naturally knew what they were doing. But one of them answered.

"It's only a tree in' it?" the boy said. "

"It's only a tree?" I retorted. "Let me tell you something. That tree is far superior to you or to me. It has been there before you were born. It will no doubt be there after I am dead and probably after you are dead. That is of course assuming that you don't kill it first. Given the law of averages, I guess that will be so."

"I tried to add a little reason to my mini speech.

"So if you think about it" I suggested "on those terms the tree is far superior to you or I. So please stop breaking branches from it okay?"

I don't know if the boys understood what I was saying. They simply looked at each other in semi bewilderment. At any rate they silently climbed down from the tree and walked away."

Clarence was looking agitated.

"That's all very interesting" he said "but what has that got to do with death?"

Stuart seized the moment to add his comment.

"Yes Brian and what about my question

about contributing to the world and then someone else taking over?"

Brian smiled. "Oh yes" he said "Don't worry I'm trying my best to answer your questions. Bear with me a while longer."

Brian re-focused his thoughts and then continued.

"At a certain season of the year I've noticed that the oak trees shed their seed. The seed or acorns as they are known lay on the ground. They lay around the base of the tree. It's my understanding that some time later the tree propagates itself."

Stuart fired a question. "Sorry Brian but what does the word 'propagate' mean?"

Brian was severed from his line of thought. He flashed his eyes towards Stuart. "Propagate?" he said aloud in a self questioning voice. "Oh yes, put simply it means to reproduce itself. In this particular case a few of the acorns managed to take root and from them little saplings have grown. They of course will eventually grow into full size trees. Furthermore they will most likely continue to live when the original tree has died. Given this basis of understanding, even if the main tree, or parent tree if you like, dies off, it hasn't totally died has it? You see, by virtue of the acorns part of the tree is growing again."

Clarence smiled. "That's very clever" he said.

Stuart was speechless.

"There's more" said Brian. "Perhaps we could liken that principle to ourselves. If we were to take a wife and have children, would we continue to live within them?"

Clarence interrupted. "But what if we didn't have any children?"

"Good question" said Brian. "My neighbours don't have children. They're married of course. But they are too old now anyway and are never likely to have children of their own. So what reason for living do they have? I believe the French expression is *raison d'être.*"

"They have good jobs and a nice house. They own a modern car, wear fashionable clothes and have frequent holidays together. All told they are generally quite comfortable. But what is the reason for them being here? Maybe when they go to places like Spain or Turkey for a holiday, they enrich other people's lives when they are there? Maybe they contribute some happiness through their influence of being there. Perhaps that is passed on to another person and to their family and so on. Maybe that's it. I guess that's what I mean when I say we contribute to the world. Who knows? "

"But let me tell you this. And maybe it is something you might like to remember. Having lived most of my life I have arrived at a conclusion. That conclusion is this. I believe that the best *things* in life are simply not *things* at all! "

CHAPTER FIVE

Another Saturday afternoon arrived. A mix of boys and girls queued outside the cinema. The gathering grew denser and longer as time passed. The children were an assortment of different shapes and sizes. In the main the girls wore gabardine raincoats over their cotton dresses. Some wore thickly woven overcoats having large round plastic buttons.

A number put on head scarves or gloves for warmth. Their hair styles varied. Some had pig-tails whilst others could be seen to wear silk bows. Both modes of fashion kept their hair in place. Boys could be seen sporting wool flannel caps. Here and there was a black beret. A choice of raincoat covered their traditional jerseys and short pants. Many wore long woollen stockings inside gum boots. Their top few inches were turned inside out. The exposed canvas lining was considered to be trendy.

Standing in groups of two or three, many jostled for prime position. They pushed and shoved but mainly argued as they impatiently waited to be let in. The mahogany entrance doors were ready to be opened but the manager was busy. He was inside his office attending to some paperwork. The cashiers who were seated inside their kiosks watched and waited nervously. The balcony was off limits. It was always kept locked during the Saturday matinee. Only the downstairs stalls were used. Janet and Suzie, the two usherettes, each waited at the entrance doors to the auditorium. They held their steel spikes with string attached, in readiness to skewer the admission tickets.

From the confines of his office the manager could hear the distant crescendo of children's voices. He checked his watch.

It was time to open the doors. The children instantly caught sight of him as he entered the foyer. A cheer rose from scores of tiny throats. The doors were opened. A rush of youngsters flooded the foyer like a giant wave crashing onto a beach. They pushed towards the cashiers with outstretched hands. Each held the few coins needed to purchase an entrance ticket.

On Saturday afternoon seats were kept unreserved. Children could sit anywhere which resulted in the rush to get inside. The usherettes struggled to collect the tickets. They tried to keep some semblance of order amongst the apparent rabble. But in spite of the chaos the seats were rapidly filled. The projectionists had been at their posts for some time. They had switched on the auditorium lighting and were playing music through the sound system. Brian had chosen a disc titled *Love Me Do*. It had entered the pop charts a few weeks earlier. It was performed by *The Beatles,* a popular music group who were rapidly climbing the ladder of fame. Music was always played before the start of a show. But the cinema had an unwritten rule. It disallowed the stopping of vocal recordings as the film began. It was considered bad form for the words to end in mid-stream. For that reason Brian made sure there was time enough for him to play his selection. It was just as well because his watch was fast approaching the magical hour of two o' clock.

The *Beatles* recording was followed by a non-vocal disc titled *Wonderful Land*. It was performed by *The Shadows* who were another popular British group. Clarence was poised and waiting next to a projector. Its lamp house was activated. He watched Brian's fingers edging the lighting rheostat downward. Through a small glass window he observed the auditorium lights. They dimmed in sympathy to Brian's moving hand.

Suddenly there was a loud rumbling sound that stemmed from within the auditorium. It sounded like a huge roll of thunder that preceded a storm. Not having heard it before Stuart nervously exclaimed, "What's that?"

"Don't worry" Brian called out "It's only the children's feet stamping on the cinema's floor boards! They do that when the film is about to begin."

Clarence grinned and calmly glanced at his watch. He saw it was precisely two o'clock. A few strands of his blond hair fell down over his face. With one hand he brushed them back into place. His other hand flicked a switch that activated the projector's electric motor. Numerous steel sprockets began to turn and drag the film from its reel. They made a loud clicking sound as they ran. Pulling a lever Clarence allowed light to escape from the lamp house. It shone through the passing film and into the lens. Images of numerals reflected from a steel plate that blocked the light's progress. The numerals flashed from seven counting down. Immediately following the last number an image of the Censor's certificate was displayed. It was the precursor to the actual start of the film. Clarence pushed another lever and the steel plate lifted. It allowed the projected images to travel across the auditorium to reach the stage. At that moment Brian activated the mechanism that opened the curtains. The certificate's image lit up the screen. Very soon it was followed by a cartoon film starring Wile E. Coyote and the Road Runner. By now the noise from the stamping of children's feet had reached a deafening level. But a second or two later, when the film was in full swing, the tiny feet had all but stopped. The cartoon film was an all time favourite. The two protagonists, Wile E. Coyote and the crazy Road Runner, waged war on each other every week. The coyote made repeated attempts to catch the ground bird. But the absurdly complex contraptions and elaborate plans to pursue his prey, often backfired on him. The coyote was hungry but the Road Runner was quick to escape his attempts of capture. His inimitable sound of 'Beep beep,' as he made good his escape, could be heard around the auditorium.

The assortment of boys and girls attending the show sat in individual seats. Collectively they formed rows stretching across the width of the cinema. The rows began near to the stage, above which the screen was suspended. They continued in alphabetical order towards the rear wall of the auditorium. To facilitate access to them was a central aisle. This was complemented by another on each opposite flank. At the left of the stage was a short narrow passage. Above it was an illuminated sign which read EXIT. The bold letters shone with a dull green light. The passage led to double doors marked FIRE ESCAPE. Next to them was the staff members' rest room and next to that the female toilets. At the right of the stage was a second short passage. It too had an illuminated exit sign. Along its length could be found another set of double doors. They too were marked FIRE ESCAPE and next to them were the male toilets.

The fire escapes comprised of two separate doors held closed by the clever use of a common 'crash bar'. The steel 'crash bar' was designed to open both doors simultaneously. When forcibly pushed it would cause the two doors to open outwards. This would prove to be a blessing in case there was a fire and the cinema had to be evacuated. But for some children the doors had another more practical use!

Pete and Mike were two young brothers. They were regular attendees. Every Saturday they would arrive early at the cinema. By so doing they were sure of getting their favourite seats. Their early arrival was usually heralded by the same weekly dialogue.

"Come on don't dawdle" Mike would say, as the two boys dashed towards Row E. They dressed in almost identical clothes. Tartan patterned long sleeved shirts were tucked into their loose fitting short pants. Popular 'snake belts', with their metallic snake-shaped buckles, kept the pants suspended. Attempting to appear trendy they wore their woollen jerseys like a kilt. The arms were knotted around their waist to serve as a belt. Placing his mackintosh over the back of a nearby seat, Mike would exclaim, "There we are! Seats numbers 9 and 10."

In like manner Pete would grumble a response.

"Don't know what all the rush is about; nobody ever wants to sit this close to the screen!"

Mike voiced a stern reminder.

"Yeah-but if we don't get these seats an' we don't do our job; we don't get free iced lollies!"

Today the two boys had gleefully watched the first cartoon film. They had laughed along with the mass of viewing children. When the second cartoon film was being shown Mike gently nudged Pete.

"Go on" he whispered "It's time to let 'em in!" He was referring to their pals who waited outside the cinema's fire escape doors.

"All right; give us a minute" demanded Pete.

Slowly, he looked around and saw hundreds of tiny heads. All were tilted slightly backwards with their eyes focused on the big screen. Each face wore an expression that varied in sympathy with the antics of the cartoon characters. Pete watched and waited. When a violent part of the film was predictably shown he put his plan into action.

He slyly slipped out of his seat. Keeping a low profile he quickly made his way to the door marked EXIT. Should anyone notice him he gave the impression he was making his way to the toilets. But once inside the short passage he bypassed them and made straight for the FIRE ESCAPE. Nervously he looked around in the subdued light to make sure he hadn't been followed. He also checked that no one was lurking in the shadows. With a concerted push his shoulder operated the crash bar. Its two heavy doors were flung open.

"Crikey you nearly knocked us over!" shouted a voice from outside. Two boys had patiently waited for fifteen minutes in the bitter cold.

"Shut up! Come in quick!" urged Pete. Without replying the two boys rushed inside. Their teeth were chattering as they felt the sudden gush of warm air. They had done this before and knew what to do. Their tiny hands felt numb and the tips of their ears ached. None the less they were glad to enter the theatre and to sit in the seats their friends had reserved.

With a little effort Pete returned the doors to

their closed position. From now onwards they looked as if they had never been touched. At the top end of the passage he listened to the sound track of the film. When he heard a violent scene causing a distraction he stealthily slipped back into the auditorium. His seat was just as he had left it. But now, sitting next to him were two additional neighbours!

The second cartoon was followed by a black and white short film titled *Malice in the Palace*. It portrayed the zany antics of what could only be described as three children in adult bodies. Individually they were called Moe, Larry and Shemp. Collectively they were known as '*The Three Stooges.*' Their slapstick and often violent humour was appreciated by the whole audience. Pete and Mike laughed out loud as they watched the three lunatics managing a café. Perhaps it would be more correct to say how they *mismanaged* the café. Some Arabs, a dog, a cat and plenty of spaghetti flavoured their riotous performance. At the end of the film came the intermission. It was announced by showing a few short animated film clips. They advertised the available refreshments using musical ditties. One proclaimed "It's time for Wall's ice cream!" Another announced "Now is the time; it's ice cream time with Lyon's Maid!"

As the last clip of film was ending the huge curtains closed to hide the screen.

The house lights slowly lit to their full intensity. Suzie, the usherette, could be seen standing in front of the stage. She held a deep plastic tray filled with various ice creams and iced lollies. It hung on a leather strap that was placed around her shoulders. The children dashed to form an irregular queue around her.

They jostled with each other for first place, just as they had done outside the cinema. Pete and Mike's two guests were amongst the small crowd. Hurriedly they bought four iced lollies. Two were for themselves and the others for Pete and Mike. The latter two would serve as payment for their arranged entry to the show.

The iced lollies were made from frozen orange juice that surrounded a wooden stick. The lolly ice was licked, sucked and slowly consumed until all that remained was the stick. For some adventurous souls the sticks were readily transformed into weapons of mass destruction. An elastic band, stretched between a forefinger and a thumb became an instant gun.

The lolly stick was bent into a vee-shape and placed across the long length of the band. Clutching the ends of the stick it was drawn back until the band came under tension. After selecting and aiming at a suitable target the assailant let it go. The bent stick would fly through the air and hit the unsuspecting victim. Cries of "Ouch" or "Who did that?" resonated around the auditorium. Fortunately for the perpetrators the shrieks of shock or pain, were drowned by the raucous cheer of hundreds of children as the second half of the show began.

The title of the main film was *King of the Range* (1947). It starred William Boyd as Hopalong Cassidy. He was a clean-cut sarsaparilla drinking hero of the Wild West. His twin pearl-handled revolvers helped him to maintain peace amongst the fractious population of the silver screen. What set him apart from other screen heroes was his apparel. Contrary to the norm he wore a broad-rimmed black felt hat and black clothing. Traditionally the good guy was recognised by the wearing of a white hat and quite often white clothing. Cassidy's two side-kicks were California Carlson and Lucky Jenkins. The former character was an 'old timer' who provided the humour in the plot. Conversely, the latter was a young handsome lad, who usually 'got the girl.' All told Hopalong Cassidy starred in sixty-six films.

The story was developing and the situation becoming tense. Pete gradually noticed his neighbour was agitated. He was moving from side to side in his seat. Not at an alarming rate but enough to distract Pete from the film. Turning his head sideways he whispered "Wot's wrong with you?"

"Nothing!" was the reply.

The agitation continued and the movement increased. Pete was distracted again and was fast becoming annoyed.

"Wot *is* wrong with you?" snapped Pete in a deeper tone.

With grimaced face the neighbour admitted "I need to pee!"

"Wot?" said Pete, hearing perfectly. "Why didn't you go to the bog when the interval wuz on?"

"I wuz busy buying your iced lolly!" was the reply.

"Well go to the bog now dumbo!" exclaimed Pete.

"I don't want to miss the shoot out" admitted the boy.

Pete looked astonished. "Well; you'ill just 'ave to do it 'ere then, won't you?"

"What do you mean?" asked the boy.

"Do it there on the floor where you're sitting!" exclaimed Pete pointing downwards.

His neighbour looked shockingly surprised.

"Do you think I could?" he whispered loudly. Pete shuddered. "Not so loud" he said. "Sure; I do it all the time."

The boy tittered and exclaimed "You don't! Yer 'avin me on!"

Pete's face took on a serious expression. He pointed to the seat in front of the boy.

"Look, just lean forward against the back of that seat.

Make like your leanin' against it. Act like you want to get a better view of t' screen. Then undo your buttons and pee on the floor. Who's gonna know?"

The boy thought about the idea. The pain in his bladder was increasing. He really had to make a choice. On the big screen Hopalong Cassidy had given an ultimatum to the 'baddies.' A shoot out was imminent. If the boy went to the toilet now he would definitely miss the best part of the show. He looked about him. Everyone within reach was intent on watching the screen. He couldn't hold his water any longer.

Following Pete's advice he tipped himself forward.

His lower arms rested on the back of the seat that faced him. His buttocks were poised on the edge of his own seat. His lower legs were tucked underneath. With one arm he supported the weight of his body. He slipped his free hand down to his fly buttons. With a little deft finger movement he managed to unfasten two of the four. Within seconds a stream of hot urine was hitting the wooden floorboards. The liquid made its way under the seats forming a pencil-line stream. It travelled like a writhing snake towards the screen.

Meanwhile Hopalong Cassidy and his side kicks were trading bullets with the baddies. Men were falling dead at regular intervals. Before long the baddies had been vanquished. All was peaceful again on the big screen. The boy too was at peace with himself. He sat back feeling relieved!

At various times during the showing of *King of the Range* the plot became tense.

Bullets from six-shooters of friend and foe flew like hailstone on a wintry day. As this was happening, it transpired that one member of the viewing audience took the film seriously.

A boy of around eight years of age had arrived at the cinema wearing an old mackintosh. His shock of dark brown hair was hidden beneath a wolf-cub cap. It represented his local Boy Scout troop. Before the main film began he had taken off his mack and rolled it up. He found that by placing it on to his seat he had a better view of the screen. Until now no one was aware that the mackintosh had kept a hidden secret. Beneath it the boy was wearing a toy cowboy gun belt. It was complete with holster and a zinc-alloy six-shooter! The belt even carried bullets placed into holders along its length. The toy revolver contained a paper roll of percussion caps. When the revolver's hammer struck a cap it let out a resounding crack along with a few sparks!

During the film, when Hopalong Cassidy was fending off the foe, the boy couldn't contain himself. He took his revolver from its holster and pointed it at the screen. He shouted aloud "Take that you varmints!" as he squeezed the trigger. The gun responded by making a loud crack and emitting a few sparks. It was heard above the audio from the film. The heads of nearby children turned to look. Suzie, the usherette, joined them. It appeared like the boy was captivated by the power of the celluloid world. He fired a second round.

"Go get 'em Hoppy" he shouted.

Suzie saw the sparks flying from the lad's gun. She made a bee-line towards him. With her torch switched on she shone its beam into the offender's face.

"Put that away this instant!" she yelled.

The young boy froze. He looked at her bewildered. It was as if he had been awoken from a dream. Suddenly he became aware of what he had done. He was foundering in a sea of remorse.

"I'm sorry miss; honest, I'm sorry!" was his cry.

Suzie saw he was repentant. She made an instant decision.

"If you make any more noise you're out! Understand?"

"Yes miss, honest!"

"I'll be watching you from a distance!"

The boy replaced his revolver into its holster and continued to watch the film. The nearby tiny faces were smiling. They had enjoyed the incident. But now their attention returned to the screen. Suzie had taken up her position at the back of the theatre. But from now on she was keeping a close eye on the young gun-slinger.

During this off-the-screen performance Suzie was blissfully unaware of yet another potential incident.

A boy was seated at the other side of the auditorium. His big brother was a member of the local Boy's Brigade. He happened to be responsible for a bugle. It was his task to play the instrument at the Brigade's weekly meetings. The young cinemagoer had borrowed the bugle without his brother's knowledge. He waited for a moment during the film when he could put it to some effect. As a regular visitor to the cinema he was familiar with films portraying the Wild West. There was often a scene when the United States Cavalry was involved. Usually they would gallop to the rescue of some unfortunate individuals. Prior to the start of their gallop a bugle was usually sounded. The boy had in mind that when the moment arrived he would duly assist the bugler. Perhaps it was just as well that in this particular film there were no scenes that required one!

87

CHAPTER SIX

The Saturday matinee had finished and the children had gone home. In their wake they had left a generous amount of rubbish. It was strewn about the auditorium's floor in random fashion. Maureen, the cleaning lady, thought it was only to be expected. There were the usual iced lolly sticks, paper wrappers and boiled sweet papers. She busily swept away the litter and generally cleaned up the mess. Her perfected system of working soon had the task under control.

The staff member's rest room, at the rear of the auditorium, measured eight square feet. Its brick walls were bare save for a coat of cream-coloured paint. Standing in a corner was a tubular steel frame. It was mounted with a porcelain sink having a singular cold water tap. Furniture comprised of a small wooden table and two stand chairs. A centrally placed electric light hung from the ceiling. A power socket and an electric kettle were added luxuries.

The usherettes and cashier ladies had

gathered there. They stood consuming cups of tea and exchanging the latest gossip.

The manager had popped out of the building. He liked to catch up on his grocery shopping in between the Saturday shows. In the meantime the projectionists had made their way down the stairs to join the ladies.

"Have you got a brew for us?" asked Brian as the three men entered the room.

"Of course we have" said Janet "And I'm going to make a special one for Stuart."

She turned to him and asked "How do you take your tea luv?"

Looking slightly bewildered he replied,

"Oh, some milk and one sugar please."

Clarence chirped up in a mocking manner.

"I'll have tea *please*. Not too much milk *please*. Oh and one and a quarter tea-spoons of sugar. *Please*."

One or two of the onlookers seemed amused. But not content to end with his request Clarence added a piece of bravado.

With some credulity he imitated Sean Connery, the film actor. He had played the role of James Bond in the newly released and highly popular film titled, *Dr. No.*

"My name is Bond, James Bond" announced Clarence. "You can make my tea shaken and not stirred Miss Moneypenny!"

The group laughed. Janet retorted somewhat indignantly, "You! you'll have it as it comes!"

Clarence parried Janet's verbal thrust by exclaiming.

"Ooh, I say; chance would be a fine thing!"

Maureen had finished her tasks and entered the rest room. She stood quietly to one side as Janet handed her a ready-made mug of tea. They exchanged affectionate smiles. Stuart was standing next to Suzie and making small talk. He was enamoured by her looks. When a cup of tea was pushed into his hand he hardly noticed.

"Drink it up before it gets cold" advised Janet.

The words shocked Stuart from his trance-like state. He gulped the tea in between sentences.

Maureen was watching the couple with discerning eyes. Stuart touched one of the plastic clips that held back Suzie's hair.

"I like your 'Beatles' hair clips" he observed.

"Oh thanks" said Suzie. "I bought them at the market place last week; they're all the rage."

"Are you a Beatles fan then?" asked Stuart.

"Well you could say that" admitted Suzie. "I've taken an interest in them since their recording of *Love Me Do* got in to the charts."

"When was that?" asked Stuart.

"Oh it was a month or two ago. October I
 think it was. It's really good you know."

"Yes. I have heard it and I do like it"
admitted Stuart.

Suzie felt at ease with Stuart. She found
him easy to talk with. The subject of pop
music was one of her favourite interests.

"Did you know they're doing a tour of the
country?" asked Suzie. "And guess what?
They're appearing at our local dance hall at
the end of the month."

Stuart recalled hearing about the visit but
he chose not to mention it.

"What?" exclaimed Stuart "The Beatles
coming to our town?"

"That's right" said Suzie, instantly feeling
important. "I'll tell you something else," she
said with growing pride. "Mi mum works in
a record shop an' she can get free tickets for
their show."

"Wow" uttered Stuart appearing to be
impressed.

"If you like" she added "We could go to see
them together?"

He thought for a second then answered.

"Sure why not."

Stuart was feeling inwardly elated. He liked Suzie a lot. "Fancy her asking me out on a date?" he thought. "What a stroke of good fortune!"

They agreed to make final arrangements when Suzie had collected the tickets.

The two lady cashiers stood side by side in a corner of the room. They reminded Brian of a pair of characters from a novelty weather forecasting-house. His mother had kept one in their home for many years. He pictured the two figures wearing appropriate dress. One holding an umbrella denoting rain was imminent. The other with a swimsuit suggesting it was to be fine. They would stand on a moving platform inside the house. The forecasted weather would determine which one would pivot outwards.

He chuckled to himself as he pictured the ladies dressed in their respective roles.

"How are you today ladies?"asked Brian as he approached them.

Together they answered. "Oh, we are not too bad thank you Brian."

Mrs. Brown took the lead. "But it's a special day for us today you know."

"Oh yes what's that then ladies?" inquired Brian.

Mrs. Brown answered. "It's forty seven years to the day when we both lost our dear husbands."

Mrs. Green added, "That was in the Great War you know." The ladies looked at each other with an air of melancholy.

"That's the First World War isn't it?" Brian asked.

"That's correct" assured Mrs. Brown.

Unable to contain his curiosity Brian asked another question.

"I hope you don't mind me asking but what happened to them?"

"Well" answered Mrs Brown hesitantly. For a second she looked at Mrs. Green as though asking for permission to answer. Mrs. Green presented a silent stoic look. She closed her eyes in a slow and deliberate blink and nodded her head. It was her sign of approval.

"It was Christmas time in the year 1915" said Mrs Brown "The British Army was engaged in building a new front line in the battle area of the Somme. They got along nicely for a time until the enemy decided to put a stop to their work." She slowly and deliberately raised her cup of tea. It reached her lips and she took a sip. With a moistened mouth she continued to speak.

"The Germans would send over a bombardment. A certain number of our men would be hit."

Unable to contain his passion Brian interrupted.

"Is that when your husbands died?" he asked.

"No, no, not then" quipped Mrs Brown "It was much later."

She deliberated for a second or two and then continued.

"Directly the bombardment ended the British would set too again building their defences. Afterwards various attacks were made and ultimately they were repulsed."

Mrs. Brown took another sip of tea. Seizing the moment of silence Mrs. Green added something of her own.

"You know" she began, "In my opinion, the attack on the Western Front without the element of surprise was wrong."

"The loss of life sustained was so great and the ground gained so small, that it never could be worthwhile."

Mrs. Brown exclaimed "I agree entirely!"

She had now regained Brian's attention.

"Anyway, as I was saying. As a result of the numerous bombardments the ground became a quagmire. Then in January of

1916 a bitter frost arrived. It froze the churned-up mud which covered the stricken fields. It became a hard crust. But the quagmire remained beneath its surface."

Mrs. Brown took another sip of tea. Brian stood transfixed and waited impatiently to hear more of her story. Mrs Brown continued.

"The roads had become quite impassable for wheeled vehicles. Ammunition was brought up to the forward guns on horses and mules wearing panniers. Unfortunately the weight of the horses was frequently too great. They would break through the crust of mud. Many of them could not be extricated."

At this moment Mrs. Brown stopped speaking. She looked down. She lowered her cup onto the saucer and held them at waist height. Brian and Mrs. Green looked on in wonder. Like a fishermen's net cast over a shoal of fish, a peculiar hush descended over the room. Leaking water dripping from the tap punctuated the silence. Droplets of water bounced off a cup sitting inside the porcelain sink. They produced a melodious note as each one struck.

Seconds later Mrs. Brown raised her head. Tears welled in her eyes. Looking momentarily at Mrs. Green she directed her gaze at Brian.

"Our husbands" she said with an emotional voice, "had been leading one such horse when it became stuck in the mud. As they were struggling to free the animal a German bombardment began. A shell exploded nearby. Our husbands were badly wounded. They died some days later."

The sound of the dripping tap returned to the room. But in addition was the sound of tinkling porcelain. It came from Mrs. Brown's cup. It rattled against the saucer as she raised them again with trembling hands.

Seizing the moment Mrs. Green spoke out.

"It is said that the enemy suffered very severely in casualties and morale. However, in my opinion in casualties the British suffered much more. They were told it was a battle of attrition and indeed it was. But I believe there was more attrition on our side than on the enemy's."

The silent onlookers appeared to suddenly re-animate. Their chatter gradually grew louder as they enjoyed drinking their tea. A few minutes later Maureen noticed that Stuart had almost finished his drink. She motioned towards Janet who wasted no time in springing into action. She interrupted

Stuart's amorous progress.

"Stuart luv" she declared. "We have a tradition at the cinema that any new employee must have their tea-cup read."

Stuart gave Janet his full attention. But he was taken aback by her announcement. He mulled over in his mind the things he had heard. Silently he mouthed the words, "Tradition"..."Tea-cup"..."Read?"

Janet sensed his apparent naivety and tried to explain some more.

"You see luv, Maureen is gifted with second-sight."

Clarence interrupted.

"Yeah, she sees everything twice. All except her pay packet!"

A ripple of laughter traversed the room.

"Clarence!" exclaimed Janet, glaring in his direction, "Be serious for a minute; please!"

She faced Stuart again and continued.

"Second sight means that Maureen is able to 'see' what is going to happen to you in the future. She does it by reading the tea leaves from your tea-cup."

Stuart looked perplexed.

"What do you mean 'reading tea leaves'?" he asked.

Janet explained. "You see luv, the idea is this. When you've drunk your tea a bed of tea leaves are left at the bottom of the cup. To the trained eye the tea leaves take on various shapes. Maureen is able to 'see' those shapes and interpret their hidden meanings. The meanings reveal future events that will happen in your life."

Stuart's expression relaxed.

"That sounds like fun" he declared.

He looked at Suzie and she nodded in an encouraging way. "All right then" said Stuart "What do we do?"

"First let me take your cup" said Maureen stepping forward. With her arthritic hands she placed the cup onto a saucer and moved over to the sink. All eyes followed her every movement. In a theatrical gesture she held the saucer level with the water tap. Lifting the cup she carefully poured the surplus liquid into the sink. The moist but firm tea leaves remained inside the cup.

"That's a waste of good tea if you ask me!" Clarence observed. Janet turned towards Clarence and frowned. "Well no one is asking you!" she blurted.

Maureen shot Clarence a glance. He was momentarily stunned. In a thrice she turned the cup up-side down on to the saucer. She gave the cup a gentle pat. As she moved the cup away the dregs of the tea leaves were left behind. Janet took the empty cup and placed it on to the sink. Maureen's hand was now free. The tea leaves lay on the saucer like an island in a ceramic sea. The onlookers formed a circle around Maureen. She turned towards Stuart. Her deep dark eyes fixed unflinchingly on his face. There was a sudden hush that descended upon the gathering.

Maureen frowned and lowered her gaze. She stared intently at the dark, moist, fragmented tea leaves. It was as if she was reading a book. Occasionally her face hinted at a change of expression. It suggested she had 'read' something of particular interest in her 'book'. At length she spoke.

"Ah," she said "I can see a church."

Turning her gaze towards Stuart she asked, "Is there anyone seriously ill in your family? Or is someone you know about to get married?"

All eyes turned away from the saucer and were now focused on Stuart. He thought for a while and finally confided that no one he knew fit into that framework.

"Well" assured Maureen "The church means there is either going to be a wedding or a funeral and you will be going to it!"

The two senior ladies turned their heads to

look at each other. They raised their eyebrows in a questioning kind of way. Maureen continued to stare at the tea leaves.

"Ah yes" she said "I can see the number 'four'. This could mean you are going to have dealings with four people at the same time." Momentarily she appeared to change her mind. "Or," she added "It could be the number of a house door."

Her facial expression suddenly changed from one of 'perhaps' to one of 'certainty.' She said "But I am sure there are people here. They are surrounding the number FOUR."

Maureen appeared to relax. She turned the saucer around once or twice. At one particular part of it she stopped. She held it closer to her eyes and then farther away. Rather like a jeweller scrutinising a diamond through an eye glass. She seemed to be focusing on something.

"Oh now I see" she announced "There is a romance here. I understand it to be a long term one. "

"It is one that begins as friendship and develops from that." Stuart felt a little embarrassed as this observation was announced. He could feel the others looking at him. As it happened they were. Suzie was no exception. Clarence looked at Janet in a romantic manner. Mockingly he pursed his lips and flashed his eye lashes. She simply glared at him in response.

Maureen continued looking at the vegetative mass. "Ah yes!" she declared, having 'seen' something else. "There is a job promotion here. Either you or a close relative is going to step up the ladder. That also suggests more money in their job."

Following this revelation Maureen became strangely quiet. She stared at the tea leaves for some time. Finally lifting her face she spoke. Her tone of voice sounded less intense. She disclosed her last revelation. "Stuart, your lucky colour is blue and Friday is a particularly special day for you."

Gradually Maureen's face perceptibly changed its demeanour. It was as though a burden had been taken from her.

"Well that's as much as I can see" she announced. "But let me add this. I can tell you that all of these things shall come to pass within a month from now."

Everyone smiled and appeared to instantly relax. Perhaps they too were relieved that the reading was over.

CHAPTER SEVEN

Suzie was thrilled when her mother gave her two free tickets to attend *The Beatle's* dance. She and Stuart had made their final arrangements to be there. Suzie had waited with growing excitement for the night of the dance to arrive. In her bedroom she stepped into a pale-blue cotton dress. It was her favourite colour. The small white flowers printed on the fabric enhanced its simple charm. A narrow white plastic belt was fastened around her waist. To buy the dress had taken half of her weekly pay. The other half had bought her black and shiny stiletto-heel shoes. A tall mirror attached to a wardrobe door reflected the image of her slender form. Music was pumping from a nearby record player. Normally it would have conveyed the sounds of *The Beatles.* After all they were her favourite musical group. But tonight it was Chubby Checker singing *The Twist*. Three years earlier the record had made the number one position in the American pop charts. It also spawned a dance craze that swept America before reaching British shores. *The Twist* had remained a firm favourite amongst all age groups ever since. Suzie's body gyrated in time to the music. She performed the mandatory dance steps. Her posture was low. Both feet were in contact with the floor. Her hips, torso and legs appeared to rotate on the balls of her feet. They moved as if they were a single unit. The shiny leather of her new shoes allowed her feet to move with ease on the carpeted floor. Her arms were bent at the elbow and held out from her body. They moved in unison with her hips.

Meanwhile Stuart lived in a seemingly parallel world. It existed a few streets distant from Suzie. He was also feeling excited following a long week of waiting. Donning his trusty Italian-styled suit and newly polished square-toed shoes he felt a sense of confidence. He remembered that he and Suzie had arranged to meet outside the *Majestic* at eight o' clock that evening. Considering they both knew the place intimately it seemed most logical. Besides it was a short walk from there to the Co-Operative Halls. And that is where *The Beatles* were expected to perform.

Muffled sounds of beat music could be heard within the two storey building. It permeated from the top of a narrow staircase that descended to pavement level. Like the literary children from Hamelin, who responded to the piper's tune, the young couple followed a stream of like-minded thrill seekers. They topped the stairs and entered the main dance hall. Suzie stared wide eyed. To her youthful outlook the hall seemed cavernous.

"Ooh it's almost as big as the cinema!" she declared.

Stuart agreed and pointed across the room.

"Yeah, an' over there is a stage!"

At the far end of the hall the stage reached to chest height. It differed from the one at the Majestic. It had no curtains and was open for all to see. A local band of musicians were standing along its edge. They played their instruments to an ever growing audience. Their music comprised of a variety of tunes borrowed from the previous decade. Elvis Presley numbers were in abundance. They were interspersed by the British sounds of *The Shadows* and Cliff Richard. All the while young people were dancing in the area to the front of them.

Non-dancers made use of the perimeter seating that followed the walls around the room. The seating was more like a continuous bench but it did provide a respite from the dancing. Unexpectedly, as if a magic spell had been cast, the band began to play the *Twist*. Almost instinctively the young couple looked at each other. "Do you want to dance?" asked Stuart.

"Of course" replied Suzie smiling broadly.

The two of them moved forward and blended into the mass of moving beings. Everyone's arms, hips and knees were in motion. Some bodies leaned forward and then backward. Others occasionally lifted a foot off the floor. At the same time they balanced their weight on the other. Then they repeated the action using their opposite foot a few seconds later. The wooden floor boards flexed in response to the dancers and the walls seemed to vibrate to the music. Envious eyes watched from the floor's outer edge. They belonged to both lads and young lasses. Collectively they harboured a mixture of feelings. Some wanted to dance whilst others wished they could dance. Some lasses waited to be asked to dance and some of the lads were too shy to ask. Stuart and Suzie were oblivious to their surroundings. They moved together in perfect time to the twanging of the guitars and the beating of the drums. Before long the *Twist* ended and was replaced by a more traditional rock and roll number. It was a copy of Bill Halley's *Rock Around The Clock*. Stuart was never at one with rock and roll music. He considered it to be before his time. Suzie was able to dance to the number but when Stuart offered to buy her a drink she didn't object. They eased their way through the growing throng of revellers.

Located behind the stage was a smaller hall. The reduced floor space was decked out with tables and chairs. Young people were sitting around in groups of twos, threes and sometimes fours. They chatted and drank fizzy soft drinks. Here and there packets of potato crisps were shared and consumed. In a corner of the hall stood a long wooden drinks bar. It presented a barrier between the resting dancers and saleable refreshments.

Stuart caught the attention of a man standing there. He ordered two bottles of fizzy drink.

"What sort do you want mate?" asked the barman.

"Have you got any sparkling Corona?" inquired Stuart.

"Sure" replied the barman. "I've got cream soda, orangeade, lemonade, limeade and cherryade. What flavour do you want?"

Stuart quickly asked Suzie to choose.

"That will be one sparkling cream soda and one sparkling limeade, please" requested Stuart. The barman placed the two bottles on the bar top together with paper straws. The young dancers sat at a table sipping their drinks through half submerged straws. The partially muted sounds of the John Barry Seven's *Walk Don't Run* could be heard streaming from the distant large hall.

Stuart watched Suzie pout her lips as she moved the tip of the straw towards her mouth. He noticed that the curved lengths of her blond hair swung towards the bottle as she drank. Her chosen shade of pale pink lipstick seemed to complement the hair. The familiar plastic *Beatles* hair clips were still in place. He felt intoxicated.

As the limeade glided up the straw and into her mouth Stuart spoke.

"So what do you make of this place then?"

Suzie swallowed the liquid and moved the bottle towards the table top.

"Oh it's really good. I never thought the place would be as big as it is."

"Yeah, it's impressive" acknowledged Stuart.

"They use the halls for different functions; like wedding receptions and funeral buffets."

"Oh really?" exclaimed Suzie "Well it certainly lends itself to those kind of things."

"So what does your dad do for a living?" asked Stuart.

Suzie deliberated for a moment before answering.

"Oh, he's a G.P.O. telephonist. You know, he's one of those people who say "Number please" when you pick up the 'phone."

Stuart sucked hard on his paper straw and raised his eyebrows in response.

"My dad works mainly night shifts at the telephone exchange" Suzie added. "There's a rule in place that doesn't allow women to work at night. But I think the union is trying to get the rule changed."

Suzie took another sip of her limeade.

"How long has he been working there?" Stuart inquired.

"Well; it's been a few years now" said Suzie as she placed her sparkling bottle onto the table. "He's quite happy at the Post Office. Although he did say that if he had enough money he would leave them and start a taxi business. He even has a name he wants to call it."

"What's that?" Stuart quipped casually.

Smiling broadly Suzie replied, 'ANYONE'.

"What?!!" exclaimed Stuart looking incredulous.

"Yes it's 'ANYONE' " assured Suzie.

"You see during the night he gets lots of calls from people wanting to book a taxi. When people pick up the phone he answers saying "Number please?"

They usually say "I want to book a taxi". Then he asks them "Which one?"

More often than not they answer, "Oh *anyone* will do". So you see that gave him the idea for 'ANYONE' taxis."

Suzie picked up the bottle again. Her lips sucked on the paper straw.

Stuart's face lit up. "Wow!" he exclaimed "That's a clever idea!"

"Yeah, he's clever is my dad" said Suzie.

She stopped to think for a second and then spoke again.

"You know he once had a strip-tease artiste who would 'phone regularly for a taxi."

Stuart pulled the paper straw from his mouth. He held the bottle in suspended animation.

"You're joking!" he said accusingly.

"No I'm not" said Suzie. "After a few calls he got chatting to her and eventually he must have gained her trust."

Stuart looked instantly puzzled.

"Why do you say that?" he asked.

"Because...." Suzie paused in mid sentence. She stared at Stuart with eyes wide open. Slowly she mouthed the words:

"Because she asked him to be her MANAGER! - Just imagine that!"

At that moment Stuart was stricken with curiosity and blurted out "Well did he?"

Suzie spoke as if she was a balloon slowly letting out its air.

"No, of course not" she retorted "he knew full well my mother wouldn't have approved!"

****

The sounds of *Wonderful Land* floated on the air. They came from the large hall and found the ears of the young couple. It was an instrumental number made famous by *The Shadows*. Both Stuart and Suzie instantly recognised it and smiled at each other. The recording was usually played at the *Majestic* before the show began. Its harmonious combination of sounds rendered it a perfect choice for the patiently waiting audience. Gradually the sounds began to fade and were replaced by a male voice. It said,

"Good evening everybody and welcome to the Co-Operative Halls."

The young people surrounding Stuart and Suzie began rising to their feet. The connecting doors between the two halls were opened. People passed through them. Everyone seemed to be heading for the main hall. Stuart called to Suzie,

"Shall we go to see what's happening?"

Suzie nodded and the two of them followed the throng.

An official looking man was standing in the centre of the stage. He spoke into a free-standing microphone.

"Ladies and gentlemen I am privileged to introduce our last group for tonight. They may be last but they are certainly not least. In fact there are four of them. They are four lads from Liverpool who have recently made a hit recording titled *Love Me Do.*"

As he spoke the swell of people was rapidly increasing. Many young lasses with a sprinkling of lads gathered along the frontage of the stage. The lasses wore a mix of knee length dresses and sported a variety of hair styles. Some had simple short cropped hair, not unlike that of school boys. Others flaunted more mature looking styles of bouffant fashion. They stood shoulder to shoulder and five deep as Stuart and Suzie arrived. Taking one look at the writhing mass Stuart called out "Let's stand to one side I'm sure we'll get a better view."

From the left of the stage they could clearly see the faces of the adoring fans. Stuart noticed a girl who was chewing gum. Her jaws moved mechanically like a cow chewing grass. Suzie spotted a girl wearing a thin roll-neck sweater. It was festooned with a pearl necklace. Instantly she made a mental note to add one to her shopping list. Together they noticed a man moving behind the announcer. He was quietly pulling a cotton sheet off a set of drums. Printed words in bold black type appeared on the skin of the bass drum. They simply read: *The Beatles.*

The man's trained hands moved stealthily amongst the various amplifiers. He methodically flicked switches and turned knobs. The announcer kept a furtive eye on him as he worked. Suddenly a quick nod from the anonymous man signalled that all was ready. The announcer smiled broadly. He half turned to face one side of the stage. His arm was outstretched in a welcoming manner. Raising his voice above the noise of the crowd he called out.

"Ladies and gentlemen without further ado I give you *The Beatles.*"

A cheer erupted from the crowd. It was intermingled with screams from numerous ladies. Four uniformed young men bounced onto the stage. Their styled and lengthy hair bounced as if in sympathy. Each wore matching clothes of light-brown suede jackets and black trousers. The ends of their trousers covered leather bootees. The sleeve cuffs of the jackets and portions of the collar were made from a darker material.

One member climbed onto a wooden plinth to reach his set of drums. He answered to the name of Ringo Starr. It was a corruption of his real name, Richard Starkey. The name Ringo had been acquired because he wore numerous rings on his fingers. Besides this he was considered to be a gifted left-handed drummer. Immediately he began to bash out a few rhythmical beats. The action was an attempt to appease the audience whilst the others made ready. They quickly connected their guitars to the amplifiers. Spasmodic electronic sounds could be heard above the noise of the crowd. The guitarists had taken up their positions and were fine tuning their instruments.

John Lennon playing rhythm guitar, stood facing the audience on their right. George Harrison playing lead guitar, stood in the centre but closer to the set of drums. Paul McCartney, with his left-handed bass guitar, stood to the left of the stage. He was in line with John Lennon. The guitarists were less than two feet from the edge of the stage. With everyone in position Lennon looked at McCartney. They both gave a hint of a nod. Suddenly John Lennon was heard to shout "One Two Three Four".

As he uttered the last syllable the three guitars burst into life. Ringo changed his tempo to blend with the latest sound. Within seconds they jointly played *Love Me Do*.

The crowd were inflamed with joy. Bodies swayed from side to side. Hands clapped and kept pace with the beat. The mouths of girls formed the words of the lyrics they heard being sung. An occasional scream was let out by an uncontrolled emotion. Stuart looked at Suzie and saw her facial expression. He was left in no doubt that she was enjoying the spectacle. He too smiled with pleasure.

Number after number was played by the talented four. *Please Please Me, Anna* and *I saw her standing there,* were all titles of songs they shared. Each and every one was played with gusto. The audience were ecstatic. The next song title to be played was called *Chains.* At that moment the outstretched arms from a number of girls could be seen. They were hoping, albeit at a distance, to make physical contact with their chosen Beatle.

By chance one pair of arms was closer than the rest. A pretty red-haired girl was wearing a grey cardigan over a green tight-fitting dress. She was standing near the front of the stage. Her horn-rimmed glasses slid to the edge of her nose as she stretched out her hand. It just managed to reach the ankle area of Paul McCartney's trousers.

The fingers of her outstretched hand closed around the fabric. They tugged on his trouser leg. Instinctively, as if he had received an electric shock, McCartney jerked back his leg. It broke free from the grip. His face grimaced as if he might be in pain. He turned his head sharply towards Lennon.

"Oh fucking hell John!" he exclaimed.

All the while the group continued to play. Stuart was inwardly shocked by this unexpected vocal expletive. His callow years had not heard much English slang and certainly never from a public figure. He looked at Suzie wondering if she had been offended. But he could see she was too absorbed by the grand spectacle to notice

Or at least she appeared not to. Like a well oiled machine the musicians worked through their routine. *Ask Me Why, There's a Place* and *A Taste of Honey* were more of the many notable numbers they played. When the title *Misery* was performed a partial sombre mood descended over the audience. But that soon changed when Paul McCartney announced *P.S. I Love You* as their following number.

Finally Paul shouted "We've reached the end of our show folks." The fans whistled and booed and many shouted "No!"

Paul simply smiled and raised his voice a little.

"The next number is our final one for the night."

The audience responded to his words with loud groans of disappointment.

"But we'd like to ask you to help us with his one" he added. "We want you all to stamp your feet and shout as much as you can. As we play *Twist and Shout!*"

At that moment it seemed like a mini earthquake had just begun.

The crowd stamped their feet on the wooden floor boards. A few of the lads whistled loudly in appreciation. Girls screamed randomly. Many called out the name 'Paul.'

The name could barely be heard above the general noise. The four guitars belched forth their powerful sound. They were nobly aided and abetted by Ringo playing his drums. All four musicians performed with maximum prowess.

John Lennon adopted a stance as though he might be riding a bicycle. With straightened back his knees were slightly bent forward. His legs were apart as if they were astride a bicycle's crossbar. The free standing microphone appeared to have been positioned too low. Lennon was obliged to hunch his shoulders so as to lower his head. He could then sing into the mike. The obligation enhanced his apparent bike riding stance.

Paul and George stood across the stage some distance away. Their opposite way of holding their guitars made it possible for them to play whilst standing shoulder to shoulder. They could also share a microphone at the same time.

"Well shake it, shake it, shake it baby now, twist and shout" cried John Lennon into his microphone. The audience went wild. He repeated the words over and over. Each time they were sung with more effort. The hair on his head bounced in sympathy to his body movement. All the while Ringo bashed out a beat on his drums. He appeared never to falter throughout the whole evening.

As the final notes of the song were strummed the audience gave a standing ovation. Anyone walking outside the building could be forgiven for thinking they were passing a football match. The audience sounds were as though a winning goal had just been scored. It took some time for everyone to calm down. They continued calling for more as the guitarists unplugged their instruments. Finally *The Beatles* formed a line and followed Ringo to the exit at the side of the stage.

In course of time the mass of teenagers began to clear from the hall. Some went to the toilets and others retrieved their coats from the cloakroom. Many more made their way towards the exits. Stuart and Suzie stood talking about the show. Occasionally someone they knew would say hello as they passed by. Two young ladies smilingly approached Suzie. They were old friends who started chatting. Stuart was introduced to them but stood for the most part saying nothing.

In an unguarded moment a stranger mysteriously approached Stuart.

"Are you one of the Beatles?" he asked in all sincerity.

What caused him to ask was never revealed. Was it the smart suit Stuart was wearing? Or was it the possible perception that he looked a little like John Lennon? Either way Stuart answered "No."

Instantly the stranger was prompted to make an announcement.

"My brother knows the Beatles and he wants me to give them a message. I'm going back stage to see them. Do you want to come along?" Stuart was taken aback. He looked instinctively towards Suzie and her friends. They had been listening to the conversation and their eyes were transfixed on the stranger.

"Can we come too?" asked one of the girls.

"No" said the stranger "There's only two people allowed to visit."

Suzie read the situation fairly quickly. She said to Stuart "You go Stuart I'll wait here for you."

"Are you sure?"

"Of course I am. It's all right. But do try to get their autographs for me if you can."

One of the girls added "And for us too please!"

"Okay. I'll try" assured Stuart.

119

"Thanks. I shall see what happens and I'll be as quick as I can."

The ladies chattered like battery hens at the prospect of Suzie's boyfriend going to see the famous four. Suzie glanced over her shoulder and caught a glimpse of Stuart in the crowd. He was following the young stranger towards a door. It was located in the short passage between the two halls. The door was closed and locked but a light glowed from a gap at its base. The stranger knocked but nothing happened.

Stuart had an idea. He produced a small notebook he always carried.

"Here, why don't you write a note on this and put it under the door?" he suggested.

"Good idea!" agreed the stranger.

A page from the tiny notebook carried the words:

"My brother knows the Beatles. He has a message for them. Please can I see them?"

The stranger slid the paper under the door and knocked again. This time a dark moving shadow disturbed the glowing light. A second or two afterwards the door opened. Light poured out from the room and illuminated the two waiting figures.

A huge man stood blocking the doorway.

The stranger recited a mini speech. He explained how his brother knew the Beatles and how he wanted to pass a message on to them. The huge man appeared not to be listening. Instead he was looking intently at the appearance of the two visitors. He looked for a second time at Stuart and pointed at him saying "Okay you can come in!"

Was it the well groomed appearance of his Italian-styled suit that tipped the scales in his favour? Stuart didn't stop to ponder. He quickly climbed up a couple of wooden steps. Passing the huge man he entered a room that was immediately behind the stage. The stranger was left behind trying to convince the huge man to let him enter.

Stuart saw various people standing about. A singular uniformed policeman, whilst wearing his helmet, stood in the centre. Surrounding him were members of the local musical group. Stuart recognised them as the ones who had played earlier that evening. They were still wearing their stage clothes as they talked and drank soft drinks. Somehow Stuart propelled himself along the floor of the cramped room. He instantly recognised Paul McCartney sitting at a small table. He was alone. His facial expression suggested that something was troubling him. Stuart's intention was to speak with McCartney but he stopped short. In line with the table was an open doorway. Beyond it was a short oblong room. Stuart glanced inside and saw three of the Beatles. They were seated on a long wooden bench. Stuart's heart was beating fast. He had never spoken to famous people before. At the far end of the bench was Ringo Starr. Stuart felt instantly challenged by his formidable appearance.

The rings on his fingers coupled with his hair style gave him a threatening look. His hair was different in style to the others. It was similar to a Teddy-boy. Stuart was familiar with the reputation of Teddy-boys. They were best known for their lack of tact. Now here he was facing someone who could possibly be a tactless person. But Stuart took a deep breath and strode towards him.

Pushing his notebook forward Stuart asked "Could I have your autograph please?"

Ringo was looking down at the floor. It was as though he was contemplating something private. Stuart's words caused him to look up. The countenance that appeared threatening quickly changed.

Ringo responded with a pleasant smile and

a singular word. "Sure."

He took hold of Stuart's notebook and asked "What's your name?" Using his own pen Ringo wrote the words "To Stuart from The Beatles, Ringo Starr."

Stuart suddenly had an afterthought.

"Oh, I'm sorry but could you please include the name Suzie?"

"Why are you called Suzie?" asked Ringo in his deep Liverpudlian accent.

"No" answered Stuart laughingly "Suzie is my girlfriend."

With that Ringo added an additional name to the written line.

"There you go" he announced.

The corrected line read "To Suzie and Stuart from The Beatles-Ringo Starr." The two shook hands and Stuart half turned to his right. He now faced George Harrison who sat quietly and without expression. Stuart repeated his earlier question. George responded politely and agreed to sign the page. Stuart turned once more to his right. Almost returning to his starting point at the door, he found himself facing the smiling form of John Lennon. The Beatle looked as though he had been waiting his turn to be asked. Stuart offered his notebook. "Could I have your autograph please?"

Appearing bright as a new penny Lennon took hold of the book.

"Sure" he said, seeming very pleased he had been asked. Using his own red inked pen he signed the book. "Did you enjoy the show?" Stuart smiled and hesitantly said "Erm, yes thanks."

He was still feeling nervous. Turning once more to his right he now faced the open door.

As he was about to walk out Lennon spoke again. Wearing a beaming smile he called out in his distinct Liverpudlian accent. He cheekily commanded, "Don't forget to buy the record!"

Stuart realised he was referring to the *Please Please Me* recording that was released just a few days before. He looked back and laughingly said "Okay."

Stuart was feeling more at ease as he now confronted Paul McCartney. The bass guitarist was still sitting at the small table and still looking worried. Stuart spoke what by now were some well practiced lines.

"Could I have your autograph please?" holding out his notebook.

The worried expression melted from McCartney's face. He immediately brightened up and said "Sure." He enjoyed the task of writing the last words on the page.

"With best wishes Paul McCartney."

Stuart was elated. His mission was accomplished.

Making his way to the exit door he was surprised to see the 'stranger' walking towards him. It seemed he had finally convinced the huge man to let him enter.

"Have you seen the Beatles?" he asked gruffly.

"Yes" said Stuart proudly. But instantly changing his tone to one of a muted apology he added "You'll find them just around this corner." He turned and pointed towards Paul McCartney's table.

As Stuart re-entered the large hall he caught sight of Suzie. She was standing where he had left her a few minutes before. Her smile was beaming as she saw him approach.

"Where are your friends?" asked Stuart.

"They've gone home. They said they were tired of waiting. But never mind about them" she blurted "Did you see the Beatles?"

"Yep" Stuart announced proudly. "And I've got something for you."

He held out his notebook for her to see. Inwardly she had an inkling of what was about to be revealed. Opening the book she saw the four Beatles' autographs displayed on the one page. They were plainly visible. Furthermore her name was with them. Suzie was over the moon. She flung her arms around Stuart's shoulders and hugged him.

"Ooh thank you soo much, you've made my day."

The dance hall was fairly empty at this time. A few pockets of stragglers could be seen talking and laughing. Stuart suggested they get Suzie's coat and make their way home. They talked about the evening all the way to Suzie's house. They even sang one or two of the Beatle's songs.

As Stuart called out "She loves you yeah, yeah, yeah" Suzie responded by singing loudly "And you know that can't be bad." They both laughed.

As they continued walking Stuart asked a question.

"Do you know something?" he said.

Suzie looked at Stuart in surprised anticipation.

"That bit Maureen said when we were at the cinema."

"What do you mean?" asked Suzie looking confused.

"Don't you remember? When we were in the rest room and I was having my tea-leaves read?"

"Oh yes, I remember but what about it?"

"Well, she said something about me meeting FOUR people, or being surrounded by FOUR people."

"Yes, well so what?" asked Suzie.

"Well I wonder if that 'Four' was the FOUR Beatles?"

Suzie looked stunned.

"Why yes, I think you might be right. How strange!"

"Yeah" said Stuart with conviction. "How strange for sure."

The couple reached Suzie's house. Standing outside the front door she looked longingly at Stuart.

"Thank you for a wonderful evening" she said. Her words were spoken with immense feeling. Leaning forward she kissed him on a cheek. Stuart felt stunned.

"Will I see you at the cinema tomorrow?" she asked.

"Er, Erm yeah, for sure" quipped Stuart standing perfectly still. Suzie waved the Beatles' autographs as she stood in the open doorway. She looked at him and whispered "See you tomorrow then. Bye."

The door closed. The spell Stuart had been under was instantly broken. He looked around and noticed the winter's frost carpeting the pavement. He hurried home. For the first time that evening he felt cold.

CHAPTER EIGHT

Clarence had a predilection for young boys. He realised his weakness years ago. It was when his parents had taken him to Blackpool for the day. An hour or two was spent on the beach where he made sand-castles. He used his small bucket and spade with amazing effect. Afterwards the family decided to have something to eat. They chose a café that specialised in the sale of fish and chips. Whilst eating a meal Clarence noted a young boy seated at the opposite table. He too was with his parents. The boy looked demure as he poked a piece of fried fish into his mouth. His delicate fingers were wrapped around an oversized fork. Clarence noted the fingernails were surprisingly clean.

In fact everything about him was clean. His dark black hair had a noticeable sheen. It seemed to reflect the fluorescent lighting that shone from above. The boy's mouth closed and he slowly chewed the fish. His eyes looked aimlessly about. That is, until they saw Clarence. He had been watching the boy for some time and trying hard not to be noticed. When their eyes eventually met Clarence was strangely excited. He felt a desire to reach out and touch the boy's hair. Disappointingly, the boy appeared blasé. He turned his attention towards the fish, which lay helpless on his plate.

Clarence realised at that moment he liked boys in preference to girls. He had 'studied' girls before but none had affected him in the same way. Working at the cinema, especially during the Saturday matinee, provided him with a golden opportunity. He could meet lots of boys who might mirror his desires.

On a wintry Saturday afternoon the Majestic's matinee was in full swing. Inside the auditorium light reflected from the silver screen. It was moving light that varied in its intensity. On the screen's surface it formed moving figures. Some were well known to the viewing audience. Characters such as *Bugs Bunny* and *Mickey the Mouse* entertained with their various antics.

Dozens of tiny faces watched intently. They appeared like bright balloons floating in a blackened sky. Some laughed and some jeered but none had noticed Clarence, who was watching from afar. It wasn't the first time that Clarence had watched young boys. He stood behind a wooden partition. It separated the stalls from a narrow passageway. Rather like a margin on the printed page of a notebook. It was designed to allow staff members to see over the top.

Having entered the passageway, from the outside foyer, any patron would be met by an usherette. She would assist the visitor to find a seat. Earlier Clarence had greeted the usherette in his usual friendly way. As he opened the foyer door he quietly called out.

"Hi Suzie how's things today?"

"Oh hi Clarence."

She recognised him as a spread of light, escaping from the foyer, had momentarily shone over his body.

"It was a bit hectic earlier but now it's settled down" said Suzie.

"I'm just checking the film's sound level" admitted Clarence.

He was attempting to justify his presence. Suzie remembered he had done this at other times in the past. She treated his visit as nothing unusual. But she had wondered why it was always *he* who came to check.

Together they looked towards the screen. Suzie smiled when she saw *Bugs Bunny;* the long eared cartoon rabbit. He stood with lanky arms and legs whilst munching a carrot. When he spoke it was with a distinctive Brooklyn accent. But Clarence was more interested in watching the heads of the numerous children. Almost at once he saw two young boys. They sat near the end of a row of seats and close to where he was standing. The seats in front and behind them were empty. In fact Clarence noted the boys were fairly isolated. But what captured his attention most was the hair of the one particular boy. It was dark black in colour. The reflected light from the silver screen gave it an enticing sheen. Clarence's thoughts returned to his day trip to Blackpool. He pictured the boy sitting in the fish and chips café. The feeling he had experienced then returned. He had the same urge to touch the hair of the boy sitting near him. "Clarence!" called Suzie quietly.

Clarence jumped. He was totally lost in his thoughts. The sudden mention of his name shocked him back to reality.

"Ye..yes" he answered.

"I've got to see the manager for a minute. Will you look after things here? I won't be long."

"Of course" Clarence said assuredly.

He smiled as Suzie walked away. She opened the door and entered the foyer. A peculiar glint appeared in Clarence's eyes. His mind was working overtime. He had prepared a mental plan for an occasion such as this. His thoughts were racing. Everything seemed to be just right. The lure of the boy's hair was too much for him. He walked stealthily behind the wooden partition. Like a panther stalking its prey in the dead of night. Reaching the end he was better placed to see the two boys.

They wore woollen jerseys above their short pants. Their long woollen stockings reached almost to their knees. But most noticeably the flesh of their thighs was exposed. Clarence was excited. His heart beat faster. The tip of his tongue protruded from his mouth. It curled slightly and licked a globule of spittle that had formed in a corner of his lips.

Reaching into his jacket pocket he took hold of a small paper bag. Glancing quickly around him he saw it was time to act. Like a peregrine falcon swooping on its quarry he moved into the row of seats.

On the screen Bugs Bunny was cavorting with Yosemite Sam. He was the antagonist who wore an oversized hat and whiskers that drooped below his chin. The two boys hardly noticed when Clarence sat next to them. But the one with the black hair sensed his presence. He looked to his side momentarily. He saw Clarence's eyes staring intently.

"Hello buddy" he whispered "Would you like a sweetie?" He offered the opened paper bag. "They're fruit pastilles" he added.

The description of the sweets made the offer more attractive.

The boy's eyes switched from Clarence to the paper bag. He saw light reflecting from the sugared surface of the sweets. They were temptation personified. His tiny hand pulled out a sparkly sugar-coated pastille.

Even in the dimmed light Clarence noticed the boy's delicate fingers. He also noticed that his fingernails were surprisingly clean.

"Does your friend want one?" he softly inquired. Without speaking the boy nudged his friend. Turning sharply the friend instantly saw Clarence.

"He's giving you a fruit pastille!" the boy

announced. Clarence was leaning across and offering the open bag. At the same time he surreptitiously slid his free arm across the space behind the first boy's shoulders.

The friend scratched inside the bag and pulled out a sparkly pastille.

"Thanks Mister!" he chirped.

His words were barely audible above those of Bugs Bunny. At that moment the cartoon rabbit uttered the classic words "Erm, What's up doc?"

Clarence had resumed his earlier position. He held the bag upright and offered the first boy another pastille. The boy was still chewing but his taste buds had succumbed to the flavour. His hand eagerly reached into the bag but fumbled. Clarence allowed his upturned hand to descend slowly onto the boy's crotch. The boy's tiny fingers followed the bag.

They grappled with a defiant pastille. Their persistence caused the alien hand to press harder onto his private parts.

During this momentary distraction Clarence's free hand slid up the boy's head. Trembling slightly his fingers gently stroked the shiny black hair. The boy's body stiffened. He sensed something was happening but he was not sure what it was.

Something was also happening inside the mind of Clarence. He became increasingly aware of his surroundings. It seemed to him that the scores of tiny faces had suddenly stopped watching Bugs Bunny. They were now watching his every move. He felt a mixture of guilt and ensuing panic. Withdrawing his arm from behind the boy he quickly whispered "Keep the sweeties buddy and enjoy."

Leaving the paper bag with the boy he exclaimed

"See you again buddy!"

He then made a hasty departure.

Within a few seconds Clarence was standing behind the wooden partition. He was trembling slightly. His eyes were sharp and opened wide. Like an owl looking for food. He made quite sure no one had followed him.

A minute or two later Suzie returned from the foyer. She approached Clarence but didn't notice his condition.

"Sorry I've been so long" she said "The manager does tend to go on a bit."

"No trouble at all" remarked Clarence whilst keeping a watchful eye on the two boys. To his troubled mind they seemed to be talking to each other.

Suzie's eyes slowly became accustomed to the low light. She began to notice beads of sweat that had formed on Clarence's forehead.

"Are you all right Clarence?" she asked.

"Yes, yes I'm fine" he replied.

Then in an attempt to distract from the question he declared

"I need to be getting back to the projection room. The lads will have my guts for garters!"

"Okay" acknowledged Suzie.

She was feeling slightly surprised by the sudden announcement.

"Well thanks anyway for keeping watch for me."

"No trouble at all" said Clarence as he made a move towards the foyer door.

Suzie watched him walk away and thought to herself "He's not as bad as they make him out to be."

CHAPTER NINE

The matinee had ended and the auditorium's lights shone brightly. The majority of the children had gone home. But two boys remained in their seats. Suzie watched as a few stragglers made their way through the exit door. She walked towards the two remainders. One appeared to be crying and the other was trying to console him. "What's the matter with you boys?" she demanded to know. The one crying managed to gargle the word "Nothing". His friend was more informative.

"'e's been touched miss."

"Shut up!" admonished the crier.

"What?" exclaimed Suzie.

"It's right miss. A bloke sat 'ere and touched 'im miss, 'onest," announced the friend.

The crier sobbed harder. Suzie was flummoxed. At that moment Janet arrived on the scene. "What's goin' on 'ere then?" she asked. When Suzie explained the situation Janet's face contorted with shock.

"I think we'd better tell the manager" she said. "I'll go and fetch him."

When Janet returned with the manager they saw Maureen sitting next to the boys. She was encouraging the crier to drink a cup of tea.

"Now then Maureen, this is no time to be reading tea-leaves" joked the manager.

Maureen was shocked by his suggestion but kept her feelings under control. "I made the tea thinking the poor lad might be in shock. And especially after what I've been told!" explained Maureen.

"Yes, yes of course Maureen, you're quite right" the manager said apologetically. He squeezed his way along the row of seats in front of the boys. He saw that the crier's nose was dripping with mucus. Tears had wetted his cheeks. The boy barely managed to sip the tea after being ardently encouraged by Maureen.

The manager reached into his jacket pocket and pulled out a handkerchief.

"Here lad" he said and offered it to the boy. "Wipe your nose before it falls off!."

The boy stiffened and glanced up. He saw the mature and kindly smile of Mister Thompson. For a brief moment the boy forgot his trouble. He accepted the gift and began to wipe his nose. Maureen took the cup of tea away.

"I'm the manager lad. You're all right now. We're are all your friends here."

The boy's water-logged eyes peered over the clenched handkerchief. He looked one way and then another at the small gathering. Suzie and Janet flashed him their sweet reassuring smiles. His friend sitting beside him pouted his lips. He firmly nodded his head in an encouraging way. The boy's eyes returned to gaze at the manager.

"It's all right" the manager said calmly "No one is going to harm you. Can you please tell me your name?"

Taking time to remember or maybe to decide if it was safe to tell, he said "It's John."

"That's good. That's a grand name; my dad was called John."

The boy attempted a smile.

"Now then John we all want to help you but I need to know a little more."

The manager leaned closer to the boy.

"What did the man look like?" he asked.

John's face instantly showed signs of terror.

"It's all right John" the manager hastily assured him. "Nothing can harm you now. Just tell me what you can remember."

The boy found comfort in the manager's words. He felt a sense of calm spread through his body.

"H..he had light h..hair" said the boy nervously.

The manager gestured towards Suzie.

"Was it as light as this lady's hair?"

"Y..yeah that's it Mister, just like that."

"Now John, can you remember what he was wearing?"

The boy was hesitant. He acted as if he was going to betray a secret. His eyes flicked from side to side as if looking for an imaginary foe. Then he spoke.

"Y..yeah; he wore a jacket and a pink coloured tie."

"A *'pink'* coloured tie did you say?"

"Yeah Mister, it was pink. An' when he offered me a bag of fruit pastilles he had to push his tie to one side."

"Oh, I see, that's good" observed the manager. "So was it fruit pastilles that he offered you?"

"Yeah, that's right.

"Did you take one?"

Hesitantly the boy answered.

"Y..Yeah Mister I did. I know I shouldn't 'ave but I did." The boy was becoming emotional. "Mi mother always told mi not to take sweets from strangers."

He began taking swift gasping breaths.

"It's all right John, It's all right. You're doing really well. You're answering the questions like a good 'un."

The boy composed himself again.

Now John we are all here to help you. But we just need to know a little more. Can you please tell me what the man did?"

"Noooo Mister, please nooo" was the boy's shrill answer. He was attempting to avoid speaking about his experience.

Janet spoke up for the first time. She said in a soothing manner

"John luv, it will really help us if you tell the manager."

The boy looked at Janet sharply. He was surprised to hear someone else speaking. He turned his head and looked at his friend. The friend nodded approvingly. The motion seemed like a silent signal that put his mind at ease. The boy looked down at the floor. He was subconsciously hiding his face and his feeling of shame. But he managed to stumble over some words.

"He sat next to me and said "Hello buddy." Then he gave me a fruit pastille."

The manager's eyebrows furrowed. He somehow managed to contain his anxiety. He wanted to confirm that which he had just heard.

"John, tell me again please, what was it that the man said?"

"He said "Hello buddy." But I didn't know him!" he whimpered.

The manager gulped; he had recognised two words. He cast a glance at Suzie. She returned the look silently and knowingly.

Without being prompted the boy continued. "I felt him touch the back of my head."

"I knew something was wrong but I couldn't move. Then I felt his hand pushing on mi willie. It wasn't my fault honest!"

The boy burst into tears again. Still holding the handkerchief, he pressed it against his face. He was trying to hide.

"It's all right John, it's all right" repeated the manager. "The man can't harm you now."

The manager had a sudden change of thought.

"All right everyone" he said, raising his voice assertively "This is what we are going to do."

Turning slightly to face John's friend he asked the question.

"Do you lads live near each other?"

The friend acknowledged that they did.

"Good" continued the manager. "I want you to take John straight home. I'm sure his mother will be starting to worry about him by now. Tell his mother what has happened and ask her to come to see me. She can come at any time the Majestic is open. Then you must go straight home yourself. Is that clear lad?"

The friend nodded his head fervently.

The manager turned quickly to Janet. "Would you please take the lads to the front door Janet and let them out?"

Like two stray lambs the boys followed, as Janet hastened to the foyer door.

The manager looked puzzled when he spoke to Suzie.

"You were on duty today Suzie. Did you see any man in the auditorium during the show?"

Suzie answered impulsively "No Mister Thompson I didn't."

A second or two later she looked confused.

"But then again I suppose I did" she added.

"What do you mean?"asked the manager.

"Well I was in the auditorium for most of the show and the only man I saw was....." Suzie froze.

"Yes! Yes! Go on Suzie!" urged the manager.

Suzie glanced quickly at Maureen. She seemed to gain strength from her presence.

"It was Clarence!" she blurted. "He was the only man I saw!"

CHAPTER TEN

Suzie's answer caused the manager distress. Thoughts tumbled inside his head like soiled garments in a washing machine. The description of 'light' hair and a 'pink' tie, as well as the words "hello buddy," were all too familiar. They could easily apply to Clarence. After all wasn't he the only man to be seen that afternoon? Within seconds the manager had reached a conclusion.

"Where is Clarence now?" he asked Suzie.
"I suppose he's in the projection room. Unless he's gone out to the cafe" she said.
"Would you please go to find him and bring him to my office?

Suzie dashed off to look for Clarence. The manager returned to his office and Maureen began her cleaning duties.

A few minutes later a knock on the office door disturbed the manager. He was reading a leaflet. It contained the synopsis of a forthcoming film.

"Come in!" he called out. The door opened slowly and in stepped Clarence.

"Ah there you are Clarence" said the

manager calmly. "Is that Suzie behind you?"

"Y..yes Mister Thompson" answered Clarence hesitantly.

"Do ask her to come in and close the door."

The two invited guests stood like two people about to cross a busy road.

"Please sit down Clarence I'd like to ask you a question or two."

Clarence sat in the vacant chair next to the door. Suzie stood near him.

The manager stared at Clarence with discerning eyes.

"Did you enter the auditorium during the matinee today?"

"Y..yes I did Mister Thompson" answered Clarence.

"Why was that?" asked the manager.

Clarence briefly looked at Suzie with an expression that seemed to say "Why is he asking me that?" Clarence answered nervously. "Because I needed to check the sound level from the film"

"I see" remarked the manager. "Now let me ask you this. During the time you were in the auditorium did you sit with any young boys?"

Clarence's face paled. He hesitated to answer. "Do you mean-*me* sit with children in the audience?"

"Yes Clarence, that's precisely what I mean."

"No Mister Thompson I certainly did not. Suzie will tell you that I spoke with *her* and then I left the auditorium."

The manager averted his eyes towards his desk. He spied the synopsis he had been reading. Staring at him from the top of the page were the words *'The Trial'*. He remembered it was a newly released film starring Anthony Hopkins. It told the story of a man who was arrested for an unspecified crime.

"Curious" thought the manager. "Was this a portent?" he asked himself.

His imagination played tricks with his mind. The office miraculously transformed into a court room. Clarence was the defendant, Suzie was the plaintiff and he was the judge. He even imagined he was wearing a judge's wig and a red coloured gown.

Clarence suddenly gave a loud nervous cough. Instantly the manager was returned to reality. Directing his attention towards Suzie he asked her a question.

"Suzie did you not come to my office during the show?"

A look of enlightenment glowed from Suzie's face.

"Why yes I did Mister Thompson. It was just

after the Bugs Bunny cartoon began."

She giggled at the thought of the long eared rabbit. Realizing the gravity of the moment she instantly stopped and apologized.

Looking puzzled the manager asked "Where was Clarence when you came to my office?"

"Well I asked him to keep an eye on things and left him in the auditorium."

Clarence was squirming in his seat. He acted like a worm. One newly dug from the ground and thrown onto a stone slab.

He was defenceless and lost.

"What do you have to say about that Clarence?" the manager asked.

Clarence kept his cool. He wasn't beaten yet. The tip of his tongue slowly protruded from his mouth. Extending slightly it turned. It licked a globule of spittle from a corner of his lips. The action allowed his mind time to think of an answer.

"Well it's true" he declared. "Suzie did leave me standing in the auditorium but that doesn't mean that I sat with any boys!"

The manager reacted with surprise at the clever answer. "Yes that's quite so" he said. He thought for a second. "But would you oblige me by doing something?"

Clarence narrowed his eyes.

"What's that Mister Thompson?"

"Would you mind emptying your jacket pockets onto my desk?" He quickly added,

"You don't have to of course but it would help me a lot. Besides, if you have nothing to fear then it won't do you any harm will it?"

Clarence paled again. He could feel his heart pounding. As he stood up he quietly muttered "I can't see what good this will do but if you insist!"

His hands slipped into his jacket pockets. Collectively he pulled out a handkerchief, a bunch of keys and a sealed paper bag. He placed them on to the desk top. Without anyone realising they rested on the printed synopsis. Curiously the paper bag almost covered the words *'The Trial.'*

The manager had seen what he was hoping for. "Sit down Clarence" he said.

"What's inside the paper bag?" he inquired.

Clarence lifted the bag and breaking its seal opened it. He held it towards the manager. In a moment of nervous levity he declared "They're fruit pastilles; would you like one?"

The manager leaned forward. He peered in the bag at the sparkly fruit pastilles. His eyes lifted towards Suzie. She looked shocked.

At that moment there was a loud knocking on the office door. An anxious voice called out.

"Mister Thompson; Mister Thompson, are you there?"

"Sounds like Janet" remarked the manager. "Would you open the door Suzie?"

Opening inwards the door came to rest against Clarence's chair. It screened him from the visitor's view. Only his knees and part of his lower legs could be seen.

Standing in the doorway was Janet. Behind her was a uniformed policeman. Next to him stood a woman with her young son.

"Sorry to disturb you Mister Thompson but these people want to speak with you."

The sight of the visitors didn't faze the manager. He had been half expecting them.

"Ask them to come in Janet" he said.

"Move over here Suzie and make more room for the people to enter."

"Oh and Mister Thompson" said Janet as an afterthought, "Just to let you know that Brian, Stuart and me are going out for something to eat."

"Yes, that's fine, thank you Janet."

The policeman entered the office. Close behind was the woman and her son who partly straddled the doorway. Removing his helmet and placing it under his arm the policeman introduced himself.

"Gud evenin' sir I'm Police Constable Moss. I've called to see you in connection with this lady. She's lodged a complaint about this cinema. I understand that you are the manager."

"Yes that's correct constable. How can I help you?"

The woman and the child stared intently at the manager. The boy's hand gripped his mother's firmly. The constable moved closer to the manager. He took a note book from a breast pocket of his tunic. Flipping it open he read from its pages.

"Well sir, this lady is Mrs. Howe and the young boy is her son. She states that during today's matinee her son was present with another young boy."

The constable looked at his notebook. He squinted at the notes written on a page.

"The name of the other boy is George Fowler. They were sitting in the auditorium when at some point during the show a man sat next to them."

Glancing briefly towards the couple the constable declared "This boy claims that the man touched him in an obscene way."

The manager studied the policeman's face.

"Do you have a description of this man constable?"

"Yes sir, I do."

The policeman read from his note book.

"The description I have states that the man was of slim build. He had fair or blond hair. He wore a pink coloured tie and spoke the words "hello buddy.""

The manager looked at Clarence. He was sitting bolt upright behind the door. The constable noted the manager's gaze. He turned his head to follow its direction. Instantly he saw a pair of protruding legs from behind the open door. To gain a better view he side-stepped a couple of paces. Scrutinizing the seated figure he suddenly realised it matched the description. His body stiffened. He gripped his helmet more firmly and looked once more at the manager.

"Do you have any male members of staff at this cinema sir?"

"Yes" replied the manager. He pointed towards the door. "One of them is sitting over there" he said.

The policeman now looked at Clarence in an accusing manner.

"Do you mind if I ask you a couple of questions sir?"

Clarence shook his head. He disguised his

fear with animal cunning. Both his fear and cunning were wound together like hair in a braid. The constable's pencil was poised over his note book. He began his questioning.

"What is your full name sir?"

"I'm called Clarence Hodgson" announced Clarence in a direct manner. As he spoke the woman and her son became aware of the mysterious talking figure. They listened, like a dog alerted after hearing a familiar sound.

"And what do you do at the cinema sir?" continued the policeman.

"I'm a projectionist" answered Clarence.

He held his head back to keep it out of sight. The woman and boy edged closer to the policeman. They wanted to get a better look at the mystery man. The boy already thought he recognised the phantom voice. The policeman's pencil was scratching words on to a page of his note book.

"And did you enter the auditorium at any time during this afternoon's show?"

Clarence almost barked an answer.

"Yes I did; but I didn't sit with any boys!"

The policeman's face looked instantly shocked. Tugging on his mother's hand the boy leaned forward. He stretched to take a peek behind the door. Finally he was able to see Clarence in his entirety. Almost at once he recognised him as his molester.

"That's 'im mum!" he screamed "That's 'im!"

The boy recoiled and tightened the grip on his mother's hand. Wrapping his free arm around her thighs he buried his face in her body. Hysterically the boy cried out "Don't let him touch me please!" The policeman bent down to console him.

The manager remained calm. His military training had kicked in. He uttered what was tantamount to a command. "Clarence!" he exclaimed. "Would you please wait outside the office and close the door?"

Clarence was wide eyed. He had the look of a fox being chased by a pack of hounds. Without speaking he pushed passed the woman and child. Once through the open doorway he pulled the door closed behind him. Standing alone in the foyer he felt a huge sense of relief. He was free from torment; at least for a while.

The boy was sobbing. The policeman spoke words of comfort. "It's all right now, it's all right. The man has gone he can't harm you." Gripping his mother tightly the boy called out "Don't let him touch me, please, please!"

The mother hugged him and spoke reassuringly.

"It's all right luv the nasty man 'as gone. This nice policeman will protect you."

The boy's face was buried in the folds of her coat. Her words calmed him down. Although still crying his curiosity got the better of him. Half turning his head he peeked at the constable. The boy's watery eye caught sight of the policeman's tunic. Light glinted from its silver buttons. He viewed them like a coy parrot from inside a cage. Again words of comfort were spoken. As calm returned to the troubled boy the policeman stood up.

"Now then Mrs Howe do you have anything to say about what has just happened?"

The woman's face looked flustered. She had been under stress for a few minutes. Sweeping her eyes over the policeman's uniform she scowled.

"My son says that 'im outside is who's dun it. I want 'im locked up!"

"I understand your feelings Mrs Howe. For the time being though, I suggest you take your son home and both of you get some rest. I shall speak to Mr Hodgson again and make further enquiries. When I have some news I shall contact you."

"Is that all you're going to do constable? 'Make further enquiries'?" cried Mrs. Howe.

"I assure you madam I shall do all I can to

find the man who committed the wrongdoing. Just leave it to me, please."

The woman felt defeated. She hugged her son in a submissive embrace.

"Suppose we'd better do what he says John. Come on let's go 'ome."

"Just a moment Mrs Howe" called the policeman.

He hastily spoke to the manager.

"Mister Thompson, would you take Mr Hodgson away from the foyer until Mrs Howe has gone? I don't want the boy upsetting again. Oh, and with your co-operation, I want to question Mr Hodgson some more."

"Yes, of course" answered the manager, moving towards the door.

As he entered the foyer Clarence was nowhere to be seen. The manager quickly looked inside the kiosks. They were empty. His curiosity caused him to look inside the auditorium. It too was empty save for Maureen. She was some distance away and sweeping the floor.

"Hello Maureen!" shouted the manager.

Maureen looked in his direction.

"Have you seen Clarence just now?"

"No Mister Thompson, he hasn't been in here."

"Okay. Thanks Maureen!" said the manager and returned to his office.

The policeman was standing in the doorway shielding the woman and the boy.

"I'm sorry" said the manager "Clarence, Erm, I mean Mister Hodgson, is not around at the moment. He may have gone to the projection room. Would you like me to go and check?"

"What I suggest sir," advised the constable, "Is to let me see these people outside and then I'll go with you."

"Very well" said the manager.

The policeman opened the mahogany door.

He watched the mother and child descend the marble steps. Holding hands they walked along the pavement. Seconds later the boy's head turned. His watery eyes saw the policeman watching from the steps. The boy's tiny face offered a smile.

CHAPTER ELEVEN

Clarence knew that Janet and the two projectionists had gone to a nearby café. He decided not to wait in the foyer.

Surreptitiously he made his way up the marble stairs. A few minutes earlier he had been sat in the manager's office. It was then that he had formulated a plan.

In the projection room he found himself gawking at a large steel hook. It was screwed into the painted ceiling. The paint was a non-reflective matt black. It was a colour that matched the surrounding walls. Years before the steel hook had been used to support a block and tackle. At that time parts of the projectors were hauled up from the street level far below. They had entered the room through an old sash window.

It was let into the outside wall. Today the window was held closed with wood-screws. Its glass panes were painted black to exclude any daylight. Clarence decided to put the steel hook to a different use.

A wooden milking-stool stood in a corner of the room. It served to sit on during the showing of a film. Clarence placed it carefully beneath the steel ceiling hook. He sat down for a while and meditated. Thoughts ambled through his head.

He remembered as a boy how heavy rain caused torrents of water to flow along the street gutters. He and his pals had played games. They placed match sticks on the fast flowing water and pretended they were speed boats. A race was held to see which match stick was the fastest. There was a time much later when he was with his father. They walked together in the countryside. His father was a kindly man and also quite knowledgeable. Sometimes he liked to share his knowledge. Clarence once asked him the question. "What is the reason for us being here?"

His father had smiled. Inwardly he had remembered asking the same question during his own lifetime. After much careful thought he answered. He believed the world should be a better place as a result of someone having lived in it. He maintained that people are born and live for a set time. Rather like the lighting of a candle. As the candle burns it produces light and heat. In so doing it radiates energy. It burns for a set time and then peters out. But when it burns out the memory of that flame lives on. He believed that the good that someone does should also live on in the world.

Clarence stood up and climbed onto the stool. He placed a leather belt around his neck and attached the end to the steel hook. Strange so it seemed, he began to hear his father's voice. It whispered gently in his ear.

The voice was heard to say "The memory of me lives on within you. For as long as you live."

Seconds later the voice fell silent. As if on cue an image floated in Clarence's mind. It was the image of a black-haired boy. He was seated in a café that sold fish and chips. The café he recalled was at Blackpool. The boy had delicate fingers that clutched an over-sized fork. He looked at Clarence and smiled. Gradually, the image faded but was replaced by another. A second black-haired boy appeared. This time the boy was seated in the Majestic's auditorium. Looking at Clarence he smiled. Slowly he raised a fruit pastille to his mouth.

Clarence lazily closed his eyes. His tongue partially protruded from his face. The tip curved slightly. It licked a globule of spittle from a corner of his mouth. At that moment he stepped off the stool. It tipped over making a loud clatter. Clarence dropped along with it. His body jerked. Thick strands of blond hair fell over his face. The leather belt swung like a pendulum from the steel hook. The belt tightened around Clarence's neck. The blood flow to his brain ceased. Clarence lost consciousness. All was dark.

****

As mother and child walked down the street, the policeman re-joined the manager inside his office. The two men faced Suzie who had been patiently waiting.

"Suzie" said the manager "Would you mind waiting in the foyer until we find Clarence?"

"Of course not Mister Thompson" said Suzie. The manager and the policeman ascended the marble stairs. They were surrounded by an eerie sense of quiet. It caused the manager to wonder where Clarence had gone. Suddenly he remembered. Janet and the two projectionists had gone to a cafe. He thought how stupid he was.

"Oh my" exclaimed the manager.

"What is it sir?" asked the policeman.

"I've just thought that Mister Hodgson may have gone to the café. Earlier Janet said she and two others were going there."

"Oh, I see" remarked the policeman.

"Would you like me to go and check?" asked the manager.

"Well, we're nearly at the top now sir. Let's first make sure he's not upstairs shall we?" They arrived at the narrow black door. The manager's hand stretched out and opened it. He felt a cold sensation cover his body. It suggested to him a presentiment that something was not quite right.

"Clarence!" he called out gruffly. There was no reply. The men climbed the wooden stairs to the top level. All was quiet save for their footsteps. Reaching the top the manager called again.

"Clarence, are you there?"

There was still no answer. All was quiet. They crossed the floor and reached the open doorway to the projection room. The two men stopped abruptly. The black sombre looking machines stood silent. Above them, hovering like some theatrical prop, was the lifeless body of Clarence. The manager froze. The policeman pushed passed him. He went straight to Clarence and took hold of a wrist. It was cold. He felt for a pulse there was none. The manger gazed at the expression on Clarence's face. There was a sense of serenity about it. He remembered seeing his wife's face in the honeymoon hotel from years before. Both expressions appeared the same. The thought of her lying in their matrimonial bed tormented his anguished mind. The constable made a sudden announcement. It shook the manager from his apparent trance-like state.

"I'm afraid he's dead sir" said the policeman. After a few seconds spent looking at the wooden stool he spoke again.

"So now we know why he didn't answer."
The manager nodded silently.

"Did I notice a telephone in your office sir?"

The manager responded hesitantly."Er, yes, there is."

"Good. Let's go down stairs sir. I'll 'phone for an ambulance."

The two men arrived at the foyer. The policeman hurried to make a 'phone call.

Suzie appeared worried.

"I'm sorry we've kept you waiting Suzie" said the manager. "Unfortunately there's been a mishap."

As he explained the situation Suzie burst into tears. She wasn't particularly fond of Clarence but the thought of him ending his life triggered her emotion. The manager tried to console her whilst ushering her into the auditorium. Maureen was still busy.

He called out, "Maureen! " She looked up.

"Would you please take Suzie to the rest room and make her some tea. I'll explain to you later what is happening."

Maureen looked puzzled but didn't question. She took Suzie by the arm and they walked away. The manager found the policeman in the foyer."The ambulance is on its way sir" said the policeman. "Where are the other staff members?"

"Two of them are in the rest room and the other three should be back any minute" said the manager. "Oh, and the two senior ladies will also be arriving. "

"Well sir, I understand the ambulance will be here within the next five minutes" revealed the policeman. "What I suggest is that you keep the foyer doors locked until it gets here. If any staff member arrives in the meantime usher them into the auditorium. It's best they don't see anything untoward."

"All right constable" said the manager "But what's going to happen to Clarence, Erm; I mean Mister Hodgson?"

"Don't worry about that sir. When the ambulance arrives the crew and me will take him away. His next of kin will be informed."

The policeman had an afterthought. "Oh, sorry sir, I'll need to take a few details from yourself if you don't mind."

"No, no not at all" replied the manager.

The sound of warning bells heralded the arrival of a cream coloured Austin ambulance. It parked outside the cinema. Two men wearing dark blue uniforms climbed out of the cab. They slammed the doors and adjusted their peaked hats. Seeing the men arrive the policeman hailed the manager.

"They're here now sir! If you unlock the foyer doors I'll speak with them."

The two men worked like clockwork toys. Methodically they opened the rear ambulance doors. From inside they took out a folded stretcher. With it was a pair of maroon coloured woollen blankets.

"If you wouldn't mind waiting here sir" said the policeman "I'll take these men upstairs. Oh and if any of your staff should arrive, it would be better if you send them into the auditorium. I'll let you know when everything is done."

"All right" said the manager.

He watched as the three men climbed the marble stairs.

CHAPTER TWELVE

The manager stood in the cinema's foyer. He stared through a glass panel of a mahogany door. In the distance stood the illuminated clock of the market hall. Its fingers registered the hour of six. On this winter's afternoon the daylight was gone. The sky was dark and the air was crisp.

Over an hour remained before the start of the next show. People stared as they passed the ambulance. Fulfilling all expectations the five staff members appeared at the entrance. The manager opened the mahogany door.

"Hello Mister Thompson" said Janet, her face beaming. "Fancy seeing you here!"

The manager forced a smile.

"We ran into the two ladies as we left the café" explained Janet. "They are a little later than usual but still in good time."

The manager stood to one side and waited until all five had entered the foyer. He locked the mahogany door behind them.

"What's the ambulance doing there?" asked Janet. The pallid faced manager ignored the question. Instead he presented one of his own. "Would you follow me quickly into the auditorium I need to speak to you all?"

The staff looked at each other with quizzical expressions. Before anyone could speak the manager had turned on his heels. He strode quickly across the foyer and held open the auditorium door. The staff members followed. Once inside they stood facing him. Their facial expressions begged for an explanation. The manager made a sombre announcement. "I'm sorry to tell you all there has been a terrible occurrence inside the cinema."

He studied the anxious faces. Toning down his voice he continued. "Clarence is no longer with us."

Stuart looked shocked. The two senior ladies were speechless. They stood with their mouths partially open. Janet looked at Brian in a way that suggested he knew something that she didn't. Brian was staring directly at the manager.

"What do you mean he is no longer with us?" Brian asked.

"I'm very sorry to tell you that Clarence has taken his own life."

"What!" exclaimed Janet looking astonished.

The two senior ladies expressed their disbelief. Almost in unison they silently mouthed the word "No!"

"What happened?" blurted Brian "I was only with him a couple of hours ago!"

As the manager explained the details to everyone, the ambulance men left the projection room. They made their way down the marble stairs. The lifeless body of Clarence was carried on their stretcher. It was covered from head to foot with the maroon blankets. A leather belt was fastened around the corpse. It held Clarence and the stretcher together. Ironically it was the belt that had taken his life.

"Mister Thompson!" cried a voice from the foyer. The sound reached the auditorium. The manager realised it belonged to the policeman. He quickly urged his staff to wait for him in the rest room. Without question they wandered slowly down the central aisle looking like lost and bewildered sheep.

Entering the foyer the manager found the three officials waiting for him. Two of them held the stretcher. Without any prompting he quickly unlocked the mahogany doors. Within a few minutes the ambulance glided away into the night. It was carrying one extra passenger.

"Will you be running a show tonight sir?" asked the policeman.

Hesitantly the manager answered.

"I think I shall discuss it with my staff first and see if they are in favour."

"Yes sir, I think that might be a good idea. And if you don't mind sir I should like to take a statement from you. But in view of the circumstances I shall call back tomorrow. Would that be all right?"

"Yes, yes, of course constable any time you like."

"Very well sir, I'll be on my way now."

The policeman descended the marble steps and into the street. After locking the mahogany door the manager hurried towards the rest room. Whilst waiting for his arrival the group had exchanged their thoughts. They were fully aware that Clarence was no longer with them. They also had mixed ideas as to the reason why.

The manager entered the room. All eyes turned towards him. The expression on his face was dour. "Hello everyone" he began.

"Thank you for waiting. I have just seen the ambulance men take Clarence away. His next of kin are to be informed."

The staff members were silent. They continued to look at the manager expecting him to say more.

"What I have in mind is this. Whatever we do will not bring Clarence back. I personally think he would want us to carry on as before. But I put this question to you all. Do you wish to continue with tonight's show or not? If anyone wishes to go home I shall quite understand."

The staff members looked at one another. Each expected the other party to say something. Their facial expressions conveyed their mood. Brian broke the silence. "Mister Thompson" he began "Since there is one man short in the projection room how will the show be run?"

The manager's countenance changed. It took on a lighter air. "Well Brian, let me say this. I think you have a worthy assistant in Stuart. Furthermore I would be quite happy to have him fill the role of Second Projectionist. What do *you* think?"

There was an instant change of atmosphere. Everyone focused their thoughts on Stuart. During the time he had been at the cinema he had worked well. No one had uttered a bad word about him. Brian thought along similar lines. As he prepared to answer he could see no visible signs of discourse amongst the group. Finally he made an admission.

"I agree with what you say Mister Thompson. I'm sure Clarence would want us to carry on without him. I for one would like to do so. And I would be happy to have Stuart help me."

The group smiled and nodded their approval. A few random murmurings confirmed Brian's answer. Janet spoke out. "Mister Thompson I think I speak for everyone when I say that we would like to carry on." She looked around at the nearby faces. All were showing their approval.

"Very well" said the manager "It's done. So let's try to put our feelings *off* and put the show *on*. Thank you all very much for your support."

Janet began to slowly clap her hands. It was her way of shedding tension and showing confidence in Mister Thompson. Her gesture was quickly copied by the others. Soon it became an ovation. The manager smiled as he turned to leave the room. When the applause petered out Janet moved closer to Maureen. She leaned forward and whispered in her ear.

"Maureen" she said.

"Yes, what is it?" asked Maureen.

Smiling confidently Janet quietly declared "It seems to me like your prediction came true!"

CHAPTER THIRTEEN

Following the meeting everyone returned to their post. The normal running of the cinema continued. Later that evening patrons began filling the auditorium and balcony. The performance began when a broad shaft of light left the projection room. It filled the silver screen with its fluctuating images. Cigarette smoke rose from the seating area. Permeating the flickering light it took on a bluish hue. Inside the projection room Brian was sitting on a wooden milking-stool. He peered through a small glass window. He was enthralled by the antics of the people on the big screen. Stuart stood next to the working projector. He watched the celluloid film flexing and bucking as it passed over the sprockets and rollers. Suddenly he was surprised by the sound of a voice calling from the outer room.

"Is anyone there?" called a female voice.

Stuart instantly recognised the voice. It belonged to Suzie. He quickly moved to the back of the room. Leaning around the machines he shouted to Brian.

"It's Okay Brian it's only Suzie looking for me!"

Brian turned his head sharply. He smiled and nodded. He fully understood Stuart's interest in Suzie and chose not to interfere. He returned to watching the movie.

As Stuart entered the outside room Suzie was standing at the top of the stairs. He thought she always looked resplendent wearing her pale-blue cotton smock.

But this time there was something different. His eyes surveyed her delicate form. Her blond hair was styled in the usual way. Likewise, the sides of her hair were held back with the help of *The Beatles* hair clips. Her pale-pink lipstick was the normal shade. It was the one that complemented her blue eyes. But something was different. The difference finally struck him. He noticed that her cotton smock was open. The vertical buttons were unfastened. Underneath she wore a dress. It was pale yellow in colour and had one special feature. Centrally placed was a vertical zipper that ran from the neck to the waist. Attached to the zipper's top was a metal ring. It was about the size of an English penny coin. Sporting a broad smile Stuart strode towards her. Suzie remained still. The look in their eyes spoke voiceless words.

"Hi Suzie what can I do for you?"

"Hi Stuart" said Suzie "The manager has sent me to ask if you would turn the sound down a bit. A couple of patrons have complained it's too loud."

"Yeah, sure" was Stuart's nonchalant reply. "For you I would do anything."

Standing directly in front of her the odour of her perfume filled his nostrils.

His eyes gazed longingly into hers.

"What's that perfume your wearing?" he asked.

"It's *Youth Dew* made by Estee Lauder. Do you like it?"

"I do" said Stuart smoothly. "I like your dress too" he added.

"Thanks" chirped Suzie.

Gradually Stuart's eyes narrowed. They caught sight of the metal ring attached to the zipper. His hand moved slowly towards it. A finger and thumb held it loosely. "What's this for?" he asked cheekily.

Suzie smiled without moving.

"That's for you to find out" she said enticingly.

Sensual thoughts entered Stuart's head. Curiosity engulfed his mind. His hand trembled slightly as his fingers gently tugged on the ring. It offered no resistance. Suzie stood steadfast. She too offered none. The zipper moved with ease on its downward journey.

"Oh; it moves!" announced Stuart sounding surprised.

Suzie smiled. The fabric of the cotton dress parted. Suzie's bare white flesh was exposed. Stuart watched his hand continue to travel. There was an uncertainty about it.

It seemed like an alien entity had taken charge. Gradually a white cotton brassiere came into view. Its presence protected Suzie's pert breasts from sight or touch. Stuart's eyes lifted and looked into Suzie's. It seemed as if he was seeking permission to continue. Her eyes looked approvingly into his. Stuart's free hand moved quickly behind her head. Breathing the fragrance of the perfume, his fingers gently stroked her hair.

Slowly the hand pulled her head towards him. With mouths closed their lips met. Instantly Suzie felt dizzy. Instantly Stuart's body tingled. Their lips parted and pressed firmly together. Seconds later Stuart's hand moved from the zipper and found its way inside the dress. It glided over Suzie's skin and lighted upon a bra-cup. Suzie's body tensed. The touch had come as a surprise. Her eyelids flickered but remained closed. She cherished the bliss of the union. They continued their kiss.

Stuart's finger-tips rested lightly on the bra-cup. Moving independently his thumb slid across the dome. It moved from left to right. Suddenly; sensing a nipple beneath the fabric it stopped. Slowly and repeatedly it stroked the tip. The nipple became firm and yet remained soft. The two lovers were intoxicated by the moment. They felt like participants in a dream. It was as if they were floating on air.

Seconds later an abrupt loud bang was heard. It came from the narrow black door. Both bodies were shocked out of their dream-like state. Suzie's eyes snapped open. They stared wildly into Stuart's. All displayed a look of shock. The bang was followed by a succession of loud footsteps ascending the wooden stairs. The two lovers were now fully alert. The magical spell was broken. The genie had jumped back into the bottle. A disembodied voice called out.

"Suzie are you there?"

Stuart realised it belonged to the manager. He was stamping up the wooden stairs. Stuart recoiled from Suzie and darted to the top of the stairway.

Looking down the stairs he called out.

"Oh hello Mister Thompson I heard you calling."

Suzie instinctively grasped at the zipper. In an instance she pulled it up. She quickly fastened her clothing.

"Hello Stuart" said the manager gruffly.

As he plodded up the last three steps he exclaimed

"I'm looking for Suzie."

"I sent her here some minutes ago."

Stuart was trying to look calm. His face was flush with embarrassment.

"Oh yes, she's here Mister Thompson. She was just on her way down."

The manager reached the top of the stairs. At that moment Suzie stepped forward.

"Hello Mister Thompson" said Suzie "I was on my way down to see you."

She too looked flushed. But she managed to hide her face in a shadow cast by the electric light.

"Stuart. Did you get my message?" asked the manager.

"Yes Mister Thompson. Everything has been taken care of."

The manager looked at Stuart in a quizzical way. He wasn't sure if he was telling the truth. He turned his head towards Suzie. Thoughts were mulling in his head. Fortunately that's where they remained.

"Come along Suzie; you need to get back to the auditorium."

"Yes Mister Thompson" said Suzie.

The manager gave Stuart a side-ways look.

"I'll see you later Stuart" he said.

Turning to descend the stairs he called out in military fashion.

"Carry on the good work. "

Suzie smiled at Stuart as she brushed passed him. She quickly followed the manager down the stairs. Stuart turned on his heels. He headed quickly to the projection room. On a wall was a control box. He hastily turned a knob to reduce the audio volume for the auditorium.

He heaved a sigh of relief.

Brian looked up from his seat. He was surprised to see Stuart standing there.

"Oh, hello again" he said as he smiled.

"Is everything all right? "

CHAPTER FOURTEEN

Down the years the number of visitors to the *Majestic* cinema had been generally constant. Although from time to time there were fluctuations in the attendance figures. But these could be attributed to seasonal disturbances such as school or public holidays. It might be said that a 'fingerprint' had been created. It was based upon the figures recorded.

At any period throughout the year a set sum of money was expected to be taken. Consequently, the financial management team, based at Head Office, would be fully aware of the cinema's monthly takings. But when those takings suddenly became less than expected, questions followed.

Falling sleet drenched the buildings and streets of northern England. The city of Manchester received its share. The sleet heralded a meeting of executive financial managers. They acted on behalf of a company named *Big Screen Enterprise*. It owned a small chain of cinemas. The *Majestic* was one of them. The Company's Head Office was located near Manchester's centrally placed Piccadilly Gardens.

Seven middle-aged men occupied an office. One sat in a corner whilst five of them sat at a polished wooden table. The seventh man stood at a window. His rotund face, with its extra chin and florid complexion, pointed towards the distant passing traffic. Hanging loosely from his corpulent frame was a pin-striped suit. Attached to a lapel was an oblong shaped plastic badge. It displayed his job title and name. The words *CHIEF EXECUTIVE - John J. Goldstein* were printed in bold black letters. Below a small Hitler-like moustache, his lips held an expensive Havana cigar. A long, narrow, wisp of grey smoke rose from its burning end. His receding hair was brushed back over his balding head. The five men had been given prior warning to attend the meeting. They had arrived in good time. As they drank cups of tea they kept a close watch on John J Goldstein. Suddenly he gave a gruff cough. The Havana cigar was almost propelled from his mouth. But his hand speedily grabbed it. His head slowly turned whilst holding the cigar aloft. His corpulent body followed. He was now facing the group of onlookers. Standing firmly in his new position he looked at their faces intently. He wore a solemn expression.

"Gentlemen" he began "I trust you all had little difficulty in finding my office?"

His voice had a certain similarity to that of Winston Churchill, the British politician.

"I hope my assistant has made the tea to your liking?" The men glanced briefly at one another. Returning their attention to the speaker they nodded in affirmation.

"I have asked you to come to my office because of a grave matter."

The expression on the men's faces morphed to one of curiosity.

Mister Goldstein spoke slowly and deliberately. He paused momentarily in-between each group of words.

"It has been brought to my attention; that the monthly monetary income; from one of our cinemas; has been noticeably reduced." The five men looked at each other in surprise. Mister Goldstein turned slowly towards the solitary man. He had been sitting quietly in a corner of the room.

"Perhaps" continued Goldstein "My learned colleague Mister Silverman, who is our Chief Financial Advisor, can explain to you in more detail."

All eyes now focused on Mister Silverman as he stood to address the audience.

His slim form with non-muscular arms contrasted noticeably with that of John J. Goldstein. Together, they might have given an acceptable impersonation of the film actors, Laurel and Hardy. Mister Silverman held a thick pad of writing paper. On it were written various facts and figures. His tempered voice thanked Goldstein for the introduction. He turned to address the seated men.

"Gentlemen, it has been my task for some considerable time, to observe the financial status of the *Majestic* cinema."

He spoke with a trace of an American accent. It may have been acquired during the years he had spent in California. It was there he had worked in the film making industry.

"As you all know" said Silverman "the monetary income for every cinema within the Company's chain, is different. But each one has its own pedigree, so to speak."

His eyes gravitated towards his note pad. They glanced at some scribbled calculations. "In the case of the *Majestic* cinema" revealed Silverman "there has been a reliable and constant in-flow of revenue."

He placed some emphasis on the word 'in-flow'. This was of course during the time I have been employed with the Company."

Silverman glanced at the ceiling as if to seek inspiration. Then he returned his attention to the audience.

"That would amount to around ten years" he confided.

He paused and drew a deep breath.

"I must say that during that time there has been an exponential growth of revenue" he added. "This I conclude is mainly due to the general popularity of cinema going."

Pausing briefly he looked directly at Goldstein expecting him to comment.

But without any words being exchanged he returned his attention to the men.

"However, in recent weeks a sharp fall in the monetary takings has been noticed."

The five men shifted in their seats. They cast a furtive glance at each other.

"Having made a close examination of the Majestic's financial spread sheets" said Silverman "I have arrived at a number of conclusions." The men stirred and murmured amongst themselves. Silverman noticed their sudden change of mood. He forced a cough to clear his throat. His voice rose slightly.

"Gentlemen!" he exclaimed. "Before I continue do you have any questions at this time?"

A singular hand was raised. A short man sporting a grey moustache called out.

"Mister Silverman, may I ask how you deduced your conclusions?"

Silverman recognised the inquirer.

"Ah yes, Mister Price isn't it?"

The man nodded.

"A very good question" acknowledged Silverman. "'Deduced' is indeed the operative word." He smiled thinly and said "Let me explain. First of all I examined the spread sheets. I found that the monetary takings for the sale of refreshments were fairly constant. Sales of cigarettes, chocolates, sweets and various ice creams were more or less unwavering."

For a few seconds Silverman looked at his note pad. He turned over a page and flicked over another. His eyes returned to the men. "Secondly I turned my attention to the sales of cinema tickets. I quickly noticed that the sum of the money taken at the kiosks, equated to the total number of tickets that were sold. But after careful inspection, I found that the reduction in monetary takings related to the balcony area alone."

Mister Price raised his hand again. Silverman stopped talking and looked at the man. His facial expression invited him to speak.

"Excuse me Mister Silverman but what prompts you to say that the balcony takings are the cause of the problem?"

"I'm about to tell you" replied Silverman whilst presenting a casual smile.

"As you all know the balcony seats command the highest admission fee."

Silverman looked directly at Price.

"Now let me ask *you* a question Mister Price."

Price pricked up his ears and sat alert.

"If the cinema sold ten tickets for the balcony and ten tickets for the stalls, which batch would command the most revenue?"

"Why the balcony tickets of course" replied Price pompously.

"That's correct" said Silverman.

He raised a hand to his tie. Due to his sustained talking the tie was causing him some discomfort. His fingers pulled on its knot to release some pressure. Feeling able to breathe more easily he continued.

"I noted that sales of tickets for seats in the stalls were what would be expected for the chosen time period. But the sales of tickets for the balcony during the same time period were *less* than expected. I further noted that the quantity of ticket stubs collected from the balcony equated to the amount of money taken! Given those facts all would appear to be above board and satisfactory."

Silverman's eyebrows narrowed. He leaned forward and stared at the audience accusingly.

"But why was there a sudden drop in attendance?" he asked. "Why were fewer balcony seats occupied? More importantly, why was there a drop in revenue? These were the questions that needed to be answered."

Everyone appeared at ease with the explanation. Price in particular approved. Observing the satisfactory look on the faces of his audience Silverman proceeded to relate his findings.

"Once the enigma of the loss of sales was discovered" he said "it was time for some remedial action to be taken."

Looking directly at Goldstein he confessed "Head Office summarily called me."

Returning his attention to the audience he continued.

"I was instructed to visit the *Majestic* cinema. But I was asked to do so discretely. This I duly did. Rather than enter the cinema immediately I secreted myself outside."

A sudden air of increased interest seemed to permeate the onlookers. Silverman picked up his pace and was beginning to enjoy sharing his experience.

"There happened to be a convenient bus shelter" he revealed. "It was situated close to the cinema's front entrance. Fortunately it afforded a magnificent view of anyone who entered the building. At this time of the year darkness had already descended. Fortunately for me it served a dual purpose. The bright lighting which illuminated the front of the cinema made for better observation. Similarly the absence of daylight allowed me to stand inside the bus shelter without being noticed. Furthermore, due to the infrequency of the buses and the small number of potential passengers, I didn't arouse any suspicion.

Of course, I might add that standing there was rather cold, to say the least".

Silverman shrugged his shoulders as if to simulate being cold.

"But the task had been given to me" he said "and I intended to see it through. So I armed myself with a simple mechanical counter."

Silverman took a small chrome plated object from his pocket. Holding it between thumb and the forefinger of his right hand he raised it to the level of his chin. Triumphantly he made a proclamation.

"This is the actual mechanical counter. It is activated by depressing the attached miniature lever."

The forefinger of his free hand rested on top of the lever.

"For every person I saw entering the building I depressed the lever once. The counter faithfully recorded the score."

Silverman's forefinger operated the lever to demonstrate the action. The counter reacted and automatically displayed an increased number. The audience looked briefly at each other. They were unanimous in their approval of Silverman's ingenuity. All the while he smiled at them. With growing confidence he said, "I followed this procedure for forty-five minutes. It began thirty minutes before the start of the cinema's show and ended fifteen minutes thereafter. I repeated the procedure at the same time every night for a month. By doing this I expected to gain a fairly accurate result." Silverman slowly returned the counter to his pocket.

"At the end of the month the spent halves of the cinema's admission tickets were collected" he said. "They were the ones held by the usherettes on their pieces of string. It was a normal procedure and therefore no suspicions were raised. The half tickets were duly counted and their total monetary value calculated."

Silverman watched the attentive faces of his audience. He looked for signs of puzzlement. Finding none he proceeded with his explanation.

"The resultant value was compared with the actual total of money collected" he said. "As expected the two sets of figures compared favourably. But when the reading on the mechanical counter was checked something was wrong. A quick analysis of the numbers showed that more people had entered the cinema than the number of tickets sold!"

With a sudden outburst of the theatricals Silverman openly proclaimed a thought.

"This discovery was tantamount to the opening of Tutankhamun's tomb!"

The audience smiled in appreciation of his imagination. Goldstein looked on sternly. Silverman saw the expression and instantly toned down his presentation.

"But even in view of all this" he said "the Management decided discretion was necessary. To be certain the information was reliable it was considered prudent to repeat the procedure using different operators. Therefore during a two month period, each week a different operator was used. "

"As it happened the results were surprisingly similar. But to quote the famous bard, it was clear that there was 'Something rotten in the state of Denmark'. Or should I say there was something rotten in the *Majestic* cinema!"

A loud guffaw erupted from the captivated audience.

Even Mister Goldstein smiled!

Outside the building a sudden gust of wind drove a torrent of sleet against the office window. It sounded like a bag of rice being emptied into a dry alloy pan. The laughter ceased. All heads turned towards the window. Mister Goldstein rose to his feet. "Gentlemen, don't worry about that" he said "We shall soon be finished and making our way home. But first I would like to thank Mister Silverman and his team for assimilating the information that he has presented to you today."

Silverman smiled and silently nodded his head in acknowledgement.

"Furthermore" continued Goldstein "I would like to inform you that Mister Silverman and I shall be investigating the matter further. Naturally, you shall all be informed of the outcome in due course of time."

Goldstein cast his gaze over the sea of faces as he thought of any point he may have overlooked. "Finally" he declared "All that remains is to thank Mister Silverman again for his input and yourselves for being present. I wish you all a safe journey home." The audience burst into spontaneous applause. Goldstein turned to face Silverman and smiled.

The executive financial managers bade their farewells and departed. The two top men stood alone. They spoke with some deep conviction.

"Now then Mister Silverman" said Goldstein whilst taking a fresh cigar from his jacket pocket.

"What do you propose we should do regarding this tiresome matter?"

"Well, I have an idea" replied Silverman. "After giving the matter some considerable thought, it is my suggestion that we go to the cinema together. I further suggest we go one evening and repeat my previous procedure."

"Do you mean we should go there with the mechanical counter? And count the number of people entering?" asked Goldstein in a surprised tone of voice.

"That's quite right sir" responded Silverman. "Furthermore, I maintain that when we have done so we should enter the building. Once inside we should repeat the internal checks. Then perhaps, and maybe then, we shall discover the truth behind this mystery."

Goldstein reached into his pocket and pulled out a gold plated cigarette lighter. The deft flicking of its mechanism caused it to produce a naked flame. Holding it against the end of the cigar he sucked like a baby on the teat of a milk bottle. In between producing puffs of smoke he spoke.

"Internal checks?" he inquired. "What do you mean by 'internal checks'?"

He blew a cloud of cigar smoke into the air as he spoke.

"Well, Mister Goldstein, I suggest we confront the cinema's manager and count the ticket stubs and the monetary takings in his presence."

Puffing on his newly glowing cigar Goldstein confirmed what he had just heard.

"The Manager?" he questioned. "That's Mister Thompson isn't it?"

Silverman nodded briskly.

"I understand he is quite reliable" declared Goldstein. "So how are we going to work this?" he asked.

"We have to do whatever it takes to resolve this matter" stated Silverman.

"May I suggest we both meet outside the cinema on Saturday evening? Say a half hour after the start of the evening's performance? "

Goldstein made a counter suggestion.

"Why don't I pick you up at your house and we can go there together?"

"That's fine sir" confessed Silverman. "That

is if you don't mind waiting in a bus shelter for an extra half hour. You see sir, I want to count the number of people entering the cinema *before* the start of the show."

"Oh, yes, I understand" said Goldstein "In that case I shall meet you outside the cinema as per your suggestion."

The two men shook hands and bade each other a good afternoon.

CHAPTER FIFTHTEEN

Saturday evening eventually arrived. Mister Silverman stood inside the familiar cold and damp bus shelter. It seemed to him like de ja vu. His heavy over coat failed to keep him warm. He wondered if the weather had grown colder since his previous visit. His eyes were firmly focused on the entrance to the *Majestic* cinema. The trusty mechanical counter was held firmly in his grip. As each member of the visiting public entered the building, he religiously depressed its operating lever.

The counter steadily advanced and indicated a generous result. It had clocked the people arriving for a full half hour before the performance began. A few sporadic late comers were also counted. Thirty minutes after the start of the show the flow of visitors appeared to have ceased.

Mister Goldstein arrived on time. A distant voice called out.

"Good evening Mister Goldstein!"

Silverman had vacated the bus shelter and was striding quickly towards him.

"Ah, good evening" was Goldstein's response. The two men shook hands.

"Are you ready for this?" he asked, whilst referring to the investigation.

"Certainly Mister Goldstein; I am."

"Shall we go in?" requested Silverman.

"Very well Mister Silverman let's go. There's no point in standing outside."

The two men climbed the three marble steps. They came face to face with the mahogany entrance doors. Light from the foyer shone through their glass panels. Silverman tugged on a large brass handle. A singular door opened. He held it as Goldstein pushed through. Seated inside the two pay kiosks were Mrs. Green and Mister Thompson. They chatted idly as a film was showing in the auditorium. On this occasion Mrs. Brown was on leave. The manager had taken her place. He usually assumed the role of cashier when there was a need. Or when he chose to do so. He suddenly caught sight of the two men as they entered the foyer. They carried official looking brief cases. His biological alarm bell started to ring. A sixth sense advised him that something was amiss. He suddenly realised the deceitful game he was playing may well be over!

Snatching a bespoke roll of tickets that lay before him, he thrust them into his jacket pocket. They were printed solely for entrance to the balcony. It was not an official roll but one for his private use.

At this moment the two visitors were standing immediately in front of the kiosk. Mister Silverman looked directly into the manager's eyes. He asked a question.

"Are you Mister Thompson, the manager?" Stuttering slightly the manager replied,

"Err, Y..yes sir I am."

"Ah, good" was the relieved response.

"I am Mister Silverman and my colleague is Mister Goldstein. We are sent from Head Office to attend to some official business. Would it be possible for us to have a word with you in private?"

The manager was reeling from the sudden intrusion to his ordered life. But gathering his wits together he replied.

"Y..yes, certainly; I'll take you into my office." He turned his head sharply towards Mrs. Green.

"Would you take care of things Mrs. Green; I must show these gentlemen to my office."

"Well of course Mister Thompson; I shall" she said.

The three men walked the short distance to the office. Entering the small room the manager beckoned the others to follow. The time it took allowed him to regain his confidence.

"Gentlemen please take a seat and tell me what I can do for you."

The two visitors sat on chairs at opposite ends of the roll-top desk. Their posture closely resembled two well sculptured book ends. The manager stood nearest the door as Silverman spoke.

"Well Mister Thompson" he began. "The directors of the cinema's holding company, that is, *Big Screen Enterprise,* have asked us to conduct an investigation."

Thompson's face looked puzzled.

"It appears that there is some concern over a reduction in the monetary income from the *Majestic* cinema."

"Oh really?" queried Mister Thompson.

His face portrayed a look of innocence.

"I wasn't aware of that" he admitted.

His manner was calm and collected.

"Yes, I'm afraid so" confirmed Silverman. "You see our financial experts have been monitoring the cash flow for some time. They are of the opinion that there can be no mistake about it."

"How very odd" added Thompson.

He continued to show surprise.

"Well; just to prove a point and in case there is some error in their judgment, would you humour us with your assistance? asked Silverman.

"Why of course" said Thompson. "What would you like me to do?"

Before Silverman could answer, Mister Goldstein, who had remained quiet up until this time, chose to speak.

"Mister Thompson, I'd like you to know that this investigation is nothing personal. We've never heard of any complaints from this cinema. In my opinion you have been doing a sterling job. But you must realise that we all have a role to play. And it's our duty to comply with the Head Office request."

Thompson looked demure as he listened to the questionable accolade.

"Why of course Mister Goldstein" the manager replied "I quite understand. I'd be glad to help in any way I can."

Silverman picked up the thread.

"Could we start by looking at tonight's takings? That is to say the money that has been collected from the total sale of tickets."

"Yes, certainly" said Thompson "I'll get the money from Mrs. Green right away."

He turned on his heels and was about to leave the room when Silverman called out.

"Oh Mister Thompson. Would you bring the ticket stubs here as well?"

The expression on Thompson's face noticeably changed as he acknowledged the request.

A short time later he returned with the money from Mrs. Green. He also carried a spike and string from the auditorium usherette. The ticket stubs festooned the string like an oriental shell necklace.

"There you are Mister Silverman" said Thompson, as he placed the items on the desk.

"The ticket stubs are from the stalls seating area. But now I must go upstairs to the balcony to get the ones from there. I'll be back in a few minutes."

As he turned to leave the office Silverman spoke.

"Thank you Mister Thompson. Oh, and would you be kind enough to send Mrs. Green to us. She can help to count the money?"

"Why certainly. I'll tell her on my way to the balcony."

Thompson hurried away. He made straight for the kiosk and exchanged a few words with Mrs Green. She obeyed his request and soon found herself helping Mister Goldstein to count the takings. Thompson darted up the marble steps towards the balcony entrance. He was nervous and excited. Adrenalin was flowing freely in his veins. He violently tugged the entrance door until it opened. In the dim light he saw Suzie standing alone. She was watching the show. He saw she was holding the spike and string. She gave a gasp as she realised the manager was suddenly standing next to her.

"Quick" whispered Thompson "Give me your tickets; I need to check them right away."

Taken by surprise and at a loss for words, Suzie allowed the manager to take the stringed ticket stubs.

"You stay here" he said "I'll bring them back to you in a while."

Thompson retraced his steps and stood outside the balcony door. In the semi-lighted area he began frantically pulling selected half tickets from the string. He chose the ones that matched his 'private' roll.

They were easily recognised by their darker colour. He tugged at the stubs like plucking feathers from a dead chicken. Hastily he stuffed them into his pocket but didn't notice when some fell to the floor. They dropped like autumn leaves from a windblown tree. He breathed stentoriously. Beads of perspiration formed on his brow.

In the manager's office the money counters were making good progress. But Silverman was painfully aware that the manager was taking, what appeared to him, to be a long time.

"I think I shall see what has become of Mister Thompson" said Silverman.

Goldstein and Mrs. Green were busy counting the money. They briefly looked at Silverman nodding their approval. Silverman set out like a bloodhound following the scent of a suspect. He darted across the foyer and ascended the marble steps. As he approached the top of the steps he was shocked to see the manager. Instantly he stopped in his tracks. He proceeded to climb at a leisurely pace. His eyes couldn't fail to notice the fallen ticket stubs. The manager froze when he caught sight of Silverman.

"Oh, are you alright Mister Thompson?" Silverman casually inquired. "We were worried that something might have happened to you."

The manager stiffened with fright. He stared wide eyed. Silverman bent down and picked up the fallen ticket stubs. He offered them to Thompson saying, "Did you drop these?"

Thompson was speechless. The blood drained from his face. Nervously he gulped. Silverman realised he had finally found the answer he had been looking for. Inwardly he cheered knowing that he was now the victor. But his outward expression gradually turned from one of triumph to one of pity.

"Come, let's go to the office" he said in a softened tone of voice. He gently motioned Thompson to follow him.

The two men entered the manager's office. Mrs. Green looked up from her seat. She appeared bewildered. Silverman asked her to leave them. He turned to Thompson and asked him to sit in the vacated chair.

Goldstein was sitting in the chair nearest the door. Silverman stood upright like a schoolmaster about to address a class. As if by some pre-arranged plan he turned towards Goldstein and nodded. The nod sent a silent coded message. Goldstein nodded in response. It signified that he understood what was about to be spoken. Silverman addressed the manager.

"Mister Thompson, you have a choice. You may either co-operate fully with us or we shall call for the assistance of the police."

Thompson was silent. His lips tightened. He looked at Silverman and simply nodded.

"Very well" said Silverman. "Please empty the contents of your pockets onto your desk."

Thompson's facial expression was like that of a puppy dog having been caught soiling a new carpet. Realising he had to co-operate he stood up. His hand reached into his jacket pocket. The fingers tightened around his personal roll of tickets. At first they refused to come out. Like a monkey's paw gripping a fruit inside a narrow-necked jar. But with some careful persuasion they magically appeared.

Mister Goldstein looked surprised. This display of deceit was something he hadn't expected.

"And now the other pocket, please Mister Thompson" requested Silverman.

Thompson repeated his previous action.

This time a handful of crumpled ticket stubs were dropped onto the desk. With a hint of some new found compassion Silverman spoke. "Thank you Mister Thompson. Do please sit down."

Thompson sat and watched Silverman fondling the half tickets and then his 'private' roll. He began to compare the serial numbers printed on them. Perhaps not surprisingly the numbers followed a sequence. The stubs had indeed originated from the 'private' roll. Silverman smiled wryly. He stood like a matador about to administer the coup de grace. Slowly he raised an arm. Like a fisherman holding a prize fish he held aloft a steel spike with its string attached. The string held some skewered ticket stubs.

"This Mister Goldstein" announced Silverman "Is what I took from Mister Thompson a few minutes ago."

Thompson's eyes were straining to see the fragments of tickets.

"Would you be kind enough to examine the string?" requested Silverman.

He presented the item to Goldstein.

"Do you see any ticket stubs that match the ones on the desk top?" Whilst holding the spike Goldstein's eyes scanned the string.

His podgy fingers touched some tickets that captured his attention. They were different in colour to the others. But more importantly they matched the colour of the manager's 'private' roll.

"Yes" answered Goldstein as he touched the tickets. "These are a match for the roll we see there."

He pointed towards the desk top.

"But what does this all mean?" he asked Silverman.

Without answering immediately Silverman turned towards Thompson.

"Would you like to explain Mister Thompson?"

Thompson simply shook his head.

"Well Mister Goldstein, to answer your question" said Silverman. "It would seem that Mister Thompson had acquired a personal roll of tickets. These were to be used solely for entry to the balcony seating. On the occasions when he was selling tickets in the kiosk, he would alternate the two rolls for the balcony."

Goldstein interrupted.

"Do you mean to say that he sold two sets of tickets?"

"Not quite, Mister Goldstein. You see he would sell a ticket from his 'private' roll to one or perhaps two people at a time. Later he would sell tickets from the cinema's genuine roll."

Sounding surprised Goldstein exclaimed "How devious!"

"In this way" continued Silverman "Mister Thompson would sell a fair number of tickets from his 'private' roll."

"But how did he manage to accrue some money?" puzzled Goldstein.

Silverman explained.

"Well since the manager had the task of reconciling the sale of tickets to the monetary takings, it was all down to him. He collected the money from the ladies in the kiosks. Then he removed his 'private' ticket stubs from the spike and string. Remember, they were all from the one string and that was used in the balcony."

Silverman was smiling freely. He could tell that Goldstein was following his logic.

"He calculated the amount of money equivalent to the 'private' ticket stubs. Then he deducted that amount from the total takings. It was the deducted amount which he pocketed."

Speaking slowly and deliberately Goldstein declared "All, very, very, clever."

Silverman turned to Thompson

"Would you agree with that explanation Mister Thompson?" he asked.

Thompson was tight lipped. He held his head down and silently nodded.

Filled with remorse he looked at his desk top. He felt empty and dejected. Perhaps ironically he considered himself a victim rather than a culprit. His eyes welled. A perfectly formed tear clung to his lower eye lid. He blinked and the tear dropped to his face. Like a rivulet finding its way along a narrow valley, the tear drop rolled slowly down the side of his nose. It stopped when it reached the tip. For a mere second it balanced precariously. It was poised like a suicide candidate standing on the edge of a high cliff. Finally the tear leapt to its destruction.

Landing on the glass of a photo frame it smashed into microns of water. They flew into the air in all directions. When Thompson's eyes cleared he saw the photograph of himself and his late wife. It had been taken on their wedding day. She was smiling at him.

Strangely, the picture became cloudy. It was replaced by the face she wore on their honeymoon. The face on that fateful morning was unforgettable. He thought what had he done? He had betrayed her memory. It was then that he sobbed.

The two visitors looked at each other. They might be hunters having shot their prey. They should have felt victorious but secretly they felt pity for their defeated foe. Goldstein looked into the face of Silverman. Unspoken words seemed to be exchanged. Turning towards the broken figure of Thompson, Goldstein spoke.

"We shall expect to hear from you soon Mister Thompson. Until then we bid you goodnight."

The visitors strode across the foyer glancing briefly at Mrs. Green. She watched them in wonderment from the kiosk. The mahogany door closed quietly as the two men returned to the cold and dark night.

CHAPTER SIXTEEN

The next day Maureen arrived at the cinema with plenty of time to spare. She liked to be sure all was ship-shape before the show began. The manager was usually there about the same time. He would unlock the entrance door. On this occasion he was late. When the other staff members arrived they were surprised to see Maureen standing there. But more so when they found the entrance door locked. Everyone huddled together on the marble steps. The temperature was colder than the day before. Attempting to allay the cold they chatted amongst themselves.

"Have you seen Mister Thompson?" Maureen asked.

"No" said Mrs. Green. "The last time I saw him was when he was sitting in his office."

"When was that?"

"That was last night after the two men from Head Office paid us a visit."

"What did they want?" Maureen asked.

"Well there was quite a fuss about the cinema tickets and the cash takings. The two men called me and Mister Thompson to his office. They wanted to check things."

"What do you mean; 'to check things'?"

"Well" Mrs. Green replied. "They seemed to be comparing the number of tickets sold with the amount of money taken. I don't know the finer points because they asked me to leave the office. But I have a feeling something was untoward."

"Did Mister Thompson say anything when the two men had gone?" Maureen asked.

"Well I seem to think he did. I mean to say when I entered his office he looked very distraught. But what he did say made little sense to me" explained Mrs. Green.

Almost begging this time, Maureen asked "So what did he actually say?"

Mrs Green thought deeply for a few moments. She struggled to remember what words had been exchanged.

"Ah yes!" she said with a smile, "I remember now."

She took a deep breath and composed herself before continuing.

"As I entered his office I saw him sitting in his chair. His head was bowed as if he was looking at the floor. I said to him "I'm ready to leave now Mister Thompson. Are you going to lock up?"

He slowly lifted his head and looked at me. His face was reddened as though he had been crying. I thought I heard him mutter "It was my gambling addiction that made me do it."

"Gambling addiction?" queried Maureen, trying to understand the situation.

"Yes, that's what I think he said" answered Mrs. Green. "But then he said something rather strange."

"What was that?" Maureen chirped.

"He looked very pitiful and said "I hope she forgives me.""

Mrs. Green gave a sigh as she asked "What do you make of that?"

"I don't know" answered Maureen "It's strange to say the least. Anyway what happened then?"

Mrs. Green paused for a moment. "Well" she said "I asked him again about locking up. This time he seemed to snap out of his morbid state and said that I could go home. He assured me that he would lock up."

Suddenly the familiar figure of Mister Silverman appeared outside the cinema. He had been watching the staff arrive from the relative warmth of his familiar bus shelter. Wearing a thick overcoat and a woollen muffler he stood at the foot of the marble steps. All eyes turned to look at him.

"Hello everyone" he said "I'm Mister Silverman. I've been sent from Head office to speak with you."

As he spoke he looked around for a familiar face. He instantly sighted Mrs Green who was standing near the entrance door.

"Ah Mrs Green, how nice to see you!" he exclaimed. He quickly climbed the steps and stood next to her. Looking back at the others he made an announcement. "I've got the keys for the entrance door. Shall we all go inside?"

Silverman side-stepped Mrs. Green and unlocked the big mahogany door. Everyone followed him into the foyer. He walked over to the kiosks and turned to look at the staff members. They gathered a few paces away. Huddled like refugees, having escaped from the cold air, their faces displayed a mix of ruddy cheeks and running noses.

"You may be wondering why I am here" began Silverman. Janet and Brian looked at each other and nodded. Maureen and Suzie stared unflinchingly. Stuart and the two senior ladies shuffled forward to get closer to Silverman.

"Earlier today" said Silverman "I spoke by telephone with Mister Thompson, your manager. He has asked me to convey his heartfelt thanks, for your loyal service during the previous months. Sadly, he has also asked me to tell you that he will not be returning to the Majestic."

There was an instant murmur of voices. The staff members were shocked by the news. They quickly fell silent in anticipation of further information.

"Mister Thompson has some private problems of which he needs to resolve.

Because of them he has decided that it would be better if he gave them his full attention. To do that he considers it better that he resigns from his post."

Silverman looked at the staff with a stone faced expression. He waited for any reaction to his words. None was forthcoming. He continued to speak.

"Until the cinema management can arrange for a suitable replacement, I shall stand-in as your manager."

He looked quickly at the staring faces hoping to detect any sign of dissension. Janet wondered what kind of person Silverman might be. But she chose not to let her face betray her thoughts. The others continued to look on expectantly.

"I should like to inform you that there is to be a funeral service for your recently deceased colleague" continued Silverman. "I believe his name was Clarence. Is that correct?" A few voices collectively uttered the word "Yes."

"The funeral service is to be held at the local Anglican Church in a few days time. If any one of you wishes to attend the service please see me afterwards for more details."

There was an audible murmuring amongst the staff. Silverman spoke again.

211

"Are there any questions you wish to ask me?"

"Mister Silverman" said Brian "What are we to do from now on?"

"What is your name?" asked Silverman.

"I'm called Brian".

"That's a very good question Brian. Well; what I would like you all to do is to go about your duties as normal. I shall be found in the manager's office should you have any queries. I expect to speak to you all individually as time moves on. So if you will excuse me, I'm sure you will want to make ready for tonight's show."

Silverman walked towards the manager's office and began to unlock the door.

The senior ladies took up their post inside the kiosks.

Janet and Maureen gravitated towards the auditorium. Stuart caught hold of Suzie's arm. He quietly spoke in her ear.

"It looks like all of Maureen's prophecies came true" he said.

"What do you mean?" asked Suzie.

"Well for one, the funeral of Clarence means I'll be going to a church doesn't it?"

"Oh yeah" admitted Suzie. "So what about the others?" she asked.

"Well there was the one about the job promotion. Didn't I get promoted when Clarence went?"

"Oh yeah" said Suzie "That's right."

"Then there was the mention of the number four or four persons" Stuart recalled. "That must have been *The Beatles* don't you think?"

"Well there's a lot of truth in that" said Suzie looking puzzled.

"Then of course there was the romance. I'm sure that must be us" suggested Stuart.

"I suppose you're right" said Suzie with a giggle. "But haven't you missed one?"

"What's that?" asked Stuart.

"What about the mention of the lucky colour blue and Friday being a lucky day?"

"You're right. I did overlook that one. But then perhaps that one is still to come."

"How do you mean?" asked Suzie.

"Well, do you think the prophecy would be fulfilled if you were to wear blue and we were to get married on a Friday?"

THE END

Lightning Source UK Ltd.
Milton Keynes UK
UKHW02f0927310718
326498UK00002B/18/P